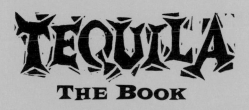

THE BOOK

# THE BOOK

BY ANN AND LARRY WALKER

ILLUSTRATIONS BY DIANE BOROWSKI

CHRONICLE BOOKS

SAN FRANCISCO

*For Anita, Carmen y Maria Luisia, who know the food in their hearts.*

Library of Congress Cataloging-in-Publication Data

Walker, Ann. 1944-
    Tequila: the book / by Ann and Larry Walker: illustrations by Diane
    Borowski
        p.    cm.
    Includes index.
    ISBN 0-8118-0288-4 (pb)
        1. Cookery (Tequila)      I. Walker, Larry. 1936-      II. Title.
TX726.W35   1994
641.6'25—dc20                                        93-31282
                                                          CIP

Book and cover design by Mitten Design.

Printed in Hong Kong.

Distributed in Canada by Raincoast Books, 112 East Third Ave., Vancouver, B.C.
V5T 1C8

10  9  8  7  6  5  4  3  2  1

Chronicle Books
275 Fifth Street
San Francisco, CA 94103

# TABLE OF CONTENTS

# A Beginner's Guide to Tequila

Tequila has captured the imagination and the palate of Americans. Interest began with the margarita and, for most people, that's the end of the tequila story. But some are learning there is tequila beyond the margarita, that a glass of tequila can be sipped and enjoyed like a fine scotch or brandy. And some are also learning what Mexican cooks have known for centuries, that tequila is very much at home in the kitchen.

This book is about tequila in the kitchen. But we haven't neglected tequila in the glass, nor the lore and legends of this intriguing Mexican tradition.

Some aficionados believe tequila is a hangover-free spirit; others are convinced that it is an hallucinogen. (Actually, the plant from which tequila is distilled is a cousin to the hallucinogenic peyote plant.) Whatever its true properties, tequila remains a distinctive, memorable spirit. We hope this book tempts you to explore tequila country beyond margaritas, both in the glass and in the kitchen.

*Salud!*

 *equilana Weber,* blue variety, is one of over four hundred known species of the agave. It is unmistakable in the field, lending a faint blue haze to the palate of the landscape. That singular blue fades into the horizon as agave rows disappear into the distance, climbing the rocky slopes of the Sierra Madre foothills in Mexico's west-central highlands. In addition to its distinctive color, *tequilana Weber* is best known as the plant from which tequila is produced.

The story of tequila, like all agricultural products, begins with the soil. The heart of the tequila zone is centered around the village of Tequila, some thirty miles west of Guadalajara, in the state of Jalisco. The soil there is a red volcanic sandy ash, with occasional patches of larger volcanic stone. Looking up from just about anywhere in the village, the jagged western reaches of the Sierra Madre form a ragged frame, producing a profound sense of isolation that leads to an awareness of the center of things, a feeling of immersion in the landscape unusual in the late twentieth century.

In contrast to the surrounding mountains, the land around Tequila is mostly flat, sliding westward toward the Pacific, about 180 miles away. There is the occasional small hill, almost always a dead volcanic cone, popping abruptly from the ground. The town of Tequila takes its name from one of those hills: *tel* means "hill" and *quilla* is the name for a kind of lava. Since the blue agave has always thrived in this area, the drink took its name from the town and the dead volcanic cone.

The spirit tequila, with its fiery flavor and explosive reputation, is well named indeed. Even more well named is the agave, a Greek word meaning "high-born." In Greek mythology, Agave, a noble woman of Thebes, was an early follower of Dionysius, the Mediterranean god of wine. Agave killed her husband, then married the King of Illyria, Lycotherses. She murdered him, too (you would think he would have been on his guard), and gave his kingdom to Cadmus, who in some accounts is reputed to have been Athena's lover. Agave is also believed by some to have been a moon goddess, which would mean she was one face of the ancient Mediterranean earth mother. Which maybe gets us back to the soils of Jalisco.

Most of the major tequila distillers are based near Tequila and the nearby village of Amatilán, so the surrounding fields

are crowded with agave. Even on a dull, overcast day, the color seems to dominate the vision, as if the land itself were a dusty blue laid over an ochre base. It's a gentle, pale blue, very like the muted blues on the ceramic pottery made by local Indians long before the Spanish arrived, or the blue of a well-loved pair of faded jeans.

Outside the agave plantations and other cultivated areas, the landscape tends toward low-growing shrubs, green and rich with wildflowers in the rainy summer season, browning in the late fall and early winter into a bronze semidesert.

Guillermo Romo (a.k.a. Bill) is the owner of the Herradura distillery. His family has owned Herradura ("horseshoe") for five generations, back to 1861. Romo, an intense man with a quick wit and an inability to suffer fools, speaks an English sprinkled with Americanisms that sound like they were lifted from old Humphrey Bogart movies. As he pulled the car to the side of the narrow blacktop road that snakes west from Guadalajara toward the coast, we surveyed the scene. There was agave growing on both sides of the road. In some fields, the young plants were only eighteen to twenty-four inches high; in other fields, older plants had reached three to four feet. The rows were planted about three feet apart, about eighteen inches between each plant, which works out to about five thousand agave plants per acre.

"My goal," Romo said, "is to establish tequila on an equal level with Cognac. And it begins right here." He waved toward the field and continued, "That's why we don't buy any agave.

I don't want some guy coming to me with a bunch of garbage. We grow about eight million plants. All of our tequila is estate-bottled, 100-percent-natural, all-blue agave. Listen, we use only the best."

Well, we can only hope that all tequila makers strive to use only the best. And, certainly, Romo's point that it all begins in the field is well taken. Of all the varieties of agave in Mexico, the blue agave is the most particular about where it grows, or at least, where it grows best, which is in rocky, volcanic soil. It also likes to keep its feet dry, so the semi-arid conditions in western Jalisco are ideal.

There is some controversy about how well it does at higher altitudes. There are enormous new blue agave plantings in Michoacán, a mountainous inland state just to the east of Jalisco, at the easternmost edge of the official tequila district and perhaps just beyond, regulatory enforcement not always being what it should be in Mexico. These plantings are between three thousand and four thousand feet in elevation, perhaps twice that of the plantations around the town of Tequila. Romo, who likes to give his competitors a hard time, is uncharacteristically noncommittal about this "mountain" tequila, saying only that he believes the mountain-grown agave "changes the flavor" of the final product. And the way he says it, you know the change is not for the best.

One of the things that makes tequila a unique spirit is the flavor of the agave, which, like wine grapes, will change under different growing conditions or in different soils. In other spirits, with the possible exception of rum, the distinctive flavors are produced in the distillation process, not from the flavor of the distilling material. (No one can really taste corn in bourbon or grain in scotch.) Even fine Cognac is far removed from the grape. So, like Burgundy from France or Rioja from Spain, fine tequila is directly linked to the land where it is made. It truly does begin with the soil. And it has only been successfully made in the tequila zone of Mexico. Somehow that unique "tequila" range of flavors seems to capture the essence of the Mexican highlands.

When we reached the Herradura distillery in Amitilán, Romo exchanged his slick city car for a four-wheel drive Jeep and we headed into the Mexican outback for a bumpy crash course in agave culture and, with luck, an agave ready to harvest.

"I'm going to show you that tequila is not cactus juice," Romo said, as he wheeled the air-conditioned Jeep onto a rutted dirt road with agave growing on either side. "I go to the United States and people tell me tequila is cactus juice, and they don't want to drink any cactus juice. I say to them, 'Listen, guy, I've lived in tequila country all my life, and I haven't seen a cactus there yet.'"

Most blue agave plants, which are actually part of the wide-spread amaryllis family, mature in eight to ten years. That may seem like a long time to wait for a harvest, but the agave isn't the only crop taken from the fields. Corn and beans are traditionally grown between the rows. This mixture of plants is a direct line to the heart of the cuisine of the west-central highlands of Mexico. Corn, beans, and tequila form a triad as distinctive as the olive-wheat-wine complex of the Mediterranean.

By the time of harvest, the bulb, or *piña* (so-called because it looks like a pineapple), may weigh as much as 150 pounds. It usually weighs nearer to 100 pounds, however, or considerably less if the plantation has not been properly maintained. The harvest goes on year round, and since the plants ripen unevenly, harvesting is not a simple matter of moving up one row and down another. It is critical to catch each plant at the right moment.

Should the ripening process progress too far, the giant, pineapple-shaped bulbs could get tough and stringy, losing some of the precious sugar that is converted to alcohol. A bulb harvested too young would not develop the intense fruit flavor looked for in a fine tequila. The harvesters, called *jimadores,* are the most highly paid workers in the field.  Catching the *piña* at just the right moment is a skill handed down from father to son, and often three generations of *jimadores* can be found working in the same field.

It becomes obvious the plant is not a variety of cactus as the agave approaches maturity. The bulb forms underground and, as it grows, forces its way to the light, eventually breaking through the earth. The tough, sword-shaped leaves protect the young *piña* as it matures, and these leaves must be cut away before the bulb is harvested.

The sugars in the *piñas* cannot be broken down except by a long heating process sometimes combined with the application of chemicals. The better tequilas are made entirely by the heating process. The *piñas* are shoveled inside huge brick-and-stone ovens and slowly cooked at a temperature of about 185°F for twenty-four hours. This cooking process softens the fibers, which are then crushed, and the extracted juice goes into large tanks for fermentation. The better tequilas—such as Herradura or El Tesoro—are fermented entirely by wild yeasts, a process that takes about 150 hours. There are artificial yeasts that do the job faster, but master tequila makers feel that some of the subtle flavors of the beverage are lost. At Herradura, some seventeen different wild yeasts have been identified. Each yeast adds a distinctive flavor element to the finished tequila.

The fermented tequila is then put into pot stills, where it is double distilled to 90 proof or higher, depending upon the individual producer. Tequila marketed with a lower proof has been cut with purified water.

Mexican regulations stipulate that tequila must contain a minimum of 50 percent distillate from the blue agave. The rest may be alcohol distilled from any source. It is possible the minimum requirement is not always met. When reading a tequila label you will find that many brands claim to be "100 percent agave." It is possible that the claim is not always true and has certainly not been true in the past. There is, however, growing concern among reputable tequila makers and importers that if regulations are not enforced, resulting scandals will hurt the tequila market in the United States. Intense pressure is being put on the Mexican government to enforce already-existing regulations.

One can only hope. For tequila at its best—as in Herradura or El Tesoro, to name two of the best and most reliable brands—is the equal of the finest bourbon, brandy, or scotch.

TEQUILA MAKERS

There are about fifty tequila producers, or *fabricantes,* in Mexico. These producers ship between sixty and seventy tequila brands to the United States, not counting private-label supermarket brands. The dominant producer is Tequila Cuervo. Its José Cuervo brand holds almost 50 percent of the U.S. market. Other reliable brands include Sanza, Montezuma, Hornitas, Jorada, and Pepe Lopez.

There are three basic categories of tequila. The silver tequilas, sometimes called white tequilas, are usually the least expensive. Often they go straight from the still to the bottle after a few weeks in stainless steel to settle them. Because of this, they maintain the fresh, intense fruit taste of the agave and are often the best tequilas to drink neat with a snack or meal, since the distinctive agave fruit complements a wide range of foods. They are also good in mixed drinks. In Mexico these tequilas are called *platas.*

The gold tequilas can be quite confusing. There are no recognized Mexican government regulations regarding their production. Some do spend a few months in small oak barrels (recycled from Kentucky bourbon distillers), but many achieve their gold color by the timely addition of caramel. Although they are often priced higher than the silver tequilas, they are rarely of significantly better quality. If they have spent time in a barrel, the gold tequilas will have a more mellow, less fruity flavor than the silvers.

The top-of-the-line tequilas are those marked *añejo*— "aged"— which means they have spent a minimum of one year in wood. This creates a richer tequila, taking away some of the intensity of the fruit but giving it a deeper feeling on the palate. These are the real class acts of tequila. Like a fine Cognac, *añejo* should be served in a brandy snifter. Sometimes *añejo* tequilas are loosely referred to as gold tequilas.

Occasionally, you see the term *muy añejo* on a label, which is supposed to mean that the tequila has been in wood for two to four years. In reality, very, very few tequilas get more than one year of barrel aging.

# Tequila at the Table and in the Glass

When it comes to tequila at the table, we are still in largely unmapped territory. Most people would agree that in the vineyard districts of the world, food and wine have grown up together. It is simply impossible to imagine basic Mediterranean cookery divorced from red wine, but tequila is the only spirit that truly matches with food. There is the odd exception, like scotch with smoked salmon or chilled vodka with caviar, but overall, no other spirit mates with as many different flavors as tequila. With its smoky base and wide range of flavors, it especially seems to wrap itself around the sauces based on chilies, particularly the silver tequilas that have much less time in wood and thus retain the fruity freshness of the agave. Tequila has a natural affinity with corn, lime, and chocolate as well.

In modern Mexico, however, it is beer that normally appears on the table. But it is there almost like water is in the United States, and the finer Mexican cooks are aware that it is tequila that better matches the intensity and richness of the Mexican kitchen. Tequila, or its country cousin pulque, has been around for centuries. As Mexican cuisine matures, the complex flavor of the agave is coming back into the kitchen. It was not ignorance that led the colonial Spanish to call mescal (the parent of tequila) vino de mescal. It was recognized that tequila (or at least the fermented or distilled liquor of the agave, whatever name it was given) belonged on the table with the local cuisine.

Most of the recipes that follow use tequila as an ingredient, but tequila also serves quite well as an accompaniment, either by itself or as a mixed drink. Mind you, we aren't talking about downing wineglass-sized servings. The flavors of tequila are so intense that a small sip will satisfy the palate. We have found that two or three ounces will carry each of us through a long meal. Most tequila is sold in the United States at 80 proof, or 40 percent alcohol, so in terms of total alcohol consumed, three ounces of tequila is equal to between nine and twelve ounces of table wine at 12 to 13 percent alcohol, or roughly two glasses.

Pulque came first. No one knows exactly when the Native Americans of central Mexico learned to brew pulque from the agave, but by the time of the Aztecs it was a fairly common beverage. Pulque is still widely drunk in Mexico. It is rarely bottled, but rather consumed by the glass directly from the barrel in small bars called *pulquerias.* It is made by tapping the juice from the agave, which then goes through a beerlike fermentation process, yielding a milky, somewhat sour-tasting beverage. Contrary to common gringo belief, it is not highly alcoholic, usually well under 10 percent.

Mescal is also made from the agave by very much the same process that leads to tequila, the most notable difference being that tequila, by law, can be made only from blue agave that grows chiefly in Jalisco and parts of surrounding states. Mescal, in contrast, is made from many different agaves in many different parts of Mexico, although the best comes from Oaxaca.

First made by the Spanish in the early 1500s, when they introduced the art of distilling to the New World, mescal is distilled from a pulque base. The better mescals can be decent enough drinks, but they never seem to have the smoothness or the depth of rich flavors found in the best tequilas.

# DRINKS

When it comes to mixed drinks, tequila is a very adaptable spirit—and a very forgiving one. Its flavors are so intense, it can carry an otherwise insipid or poorly balanced drink, such as a recipe that combines tequila with grapes, bananas, rum, mint, and some other stuff that you don't want to know about or ever taste.

The following drinks recipes will get you started. After you have mastered them, you are on your own. Just start with a good bottle of tequila, some limes, some oranges, perhaps a bottle of Triple Sec or other orange liqueur, and let your imagination run wild.

The margarita is the way most Americans first meet tequila, yet the introduction has rarely been properly made. Most margaritas look like a snow cone in a glass. The temptation is to ask for a spoon or to pour chocolate sauce over it. On the other hand, there might be some justification for the frozen approach. The ice-cold drink can deaden the taste buds to the point where it is impossible to taste the questionable liquid that passes for tequila in many bars and on supermarket shelves.

The drink clearly comes from the traditional Mexican way of drinking tequila neat, with a pinch of salt on the palm of the hand and half a lime between thumb and forefinger. No one knows for sure who first thought of putting those ingredients in a glass and adding the Triple Sec, although plenty of people claim the honor.

The earliest date put forward is about 1930, in two different places, an obscure bar in Taxco and the bar at the Caliente Race Track in Tijuana. Yet another historical faction claims it was invented at the Hotel Garci Crespo in Puebla in 1936. Although questions certainly remain unanswered about the birthplace of the margarita, there is good reason to believe that it first crossed the border in the early 1950s and turned up at a bar in Los Angeles called The Tail of the Cock.

The origin of the name is as obscure as the drink, although most of the stories quite properly involve a beautiful Mexican woman named Margarita and a bartender who tried to win her heart by inventing a drink in her honor. Almost every one of those tales has a happy ending.

# THE PERFECT MARGARITA
## *La Margarita Definitiva*

 Serves 1

The perfect margarita is as simple as can be—just shun any prepared margarita mix and use a good-quality tequila. A silver tequila will produce a fruity, fresh-tasting margarita, while an *añejo* tequila makes a rounder, more complex drink. Salt the rim of the glass as you wish, but bear in mind that the salt will mask the taste of the tequila. Chilled glasses make a nice touch, although they have little effect on the drink. And, please, no crushed-ice, snow-cone margaritas.

> *1½ ounces tequila*
> *½ ounce Triple Sec*
> *1 ounce fresh lime juice*

Combine all the ingredients in a cocktail shaker and shake well. Pour into a glass and serve without garnish, unless you are in Las Vegas where garnish is mandatory, then the more outlandish the better. Repeat as needed.

**PASS THE SALT**

 If you wish to salt the rim of your margarita glass, the best method is as follows: Sprinkle a few tablespoons of salt on a dry paper towel. Wet the rim of your empty glass and turn it upside down on the salt, giving it a few twists to distribute the salt around the rim. A coarse-grained salt, such as a kosher salt or a medium sea salt, works well.

# JULIO'S SANGRITA
*Needs No Translation, Just Drink It*

 SERVES 6

There are dozens of variations on *sangrita,* the tomato juice–based drink that is often served with a glass of straight tequila. Some call for orange juice or grenadine, even pineapple juice. We found our favorite in San Francisco at Tommy's Mexican Restaurant. Bartender Julio Bermejo, the son of restaurant founder Tommy Bermejo, gave us this recipe. Although not traditional, many drinkers combine the tequila and the tomato mixture and sip rather than "shoot" them. If you do combine them, cut back by about one half on the tequila and the other flavors will come forward.

> *²/₃ cup tomato juice*
> *½ teaspoon salt*
> *½ teaspoon freshly ground black pepper*
> *14 dashes Tabasco sauce (about 1½ teaspoons)*
> *1½ tablespoons fresh lime juice (about 1½ limes)*
> *6 ounces good-quality silver tequila*

In a small pitcher, stir together the tomato juice, salt, pepper, Tabasco, and lime juice. Pour into 6 shot glasses. Fill 6 more shot glasses with the tequila. Serve a glass of each to each guest.

# TEQUILA OYSTER SHOTS
### Chupitos de Tequila con Ostiones

SERVES 8

This was probably developed at some seaside resort for the gringo crowd, but that doesn't keep it from being delicious. A few of these served to guests as a cocktail will get the party rolling nicely.

> *8 small oysters in the shell, shucked*
> *4 teaspoons fresh lime juice*
> *salt*
> *8 dashes Tabasco sauce, or 4 teaspoons Tomatillo Salsa*
>    *(see page 103)*
> *good-quality silver tequila*

Divide the oysters among 8 shot glasses. Pour ½ teaspoon of the lime juice over each oyster. Sprinkle each oyster lightly with salt and a dash of Tabasco or ½ teaspoon of the Tomatillo Salsa. Fill each glass to the brim with tequila. Drink in one gulp. Savor. Repeat as needed.

# GOOD MORNING, AMERICA, HOW ARE YOU?

*Buenos Días, Gringo, Como Ésta?*

 SERVES 1

A good friend of ours and fellow Mexican-food nut, Al Dollberg, invented this variation on the classic tequila sunrise. He came up with it one morning at the beach when he discovered that we don't stock grenadine in our liquor cabinet, but we did have Triple Sec left over from making margaritas the day before. We like Al's version better than the original and have made it his way ever since.

> *2 ounces silver tequila*
> *½ ounce fresh lime juice*
> *3 ounces fresh orange juice*
> *½ ounce Triple Sec*
> *crushed ice*
> *lime slice*
> *club soda (optional)*

Combine the tequila, lime juice, orange juice, and Triple Sec in a cocktail shaker and shake well. Half-fill a tall glass (about 12 ounces) with crushed ice. Pour in the tequila mixture. Garnish with the slice of lime. If you wish, top off the glass with club soda. Repeat as needed.

# THE TEQUILA SHOT

SERVES 1

Tequila, lime, salt. The basic tequila shot, the origins lost deep in Tijuana *cantina macho*. There is endless debate about the order of those three ingredients. Some go for salt, lime, and tequila; some for lime, salt, and tequila. We started taking the tequila up front so we could enjoy its taste more. You can experiment and see how you like it best. Always use good tequila and don't lose count of how many shots you've had. It could be dangerous.

> *1 ounce tequila*
> *pinch of salt*
> *lime slice*

Pour the tequila into a shot glass. Lick the flap of skin between thumb and forefinger and put salt on the moist skin. Drink the tequila, lick the salt, and suck on the lime.

Repeat as needed. Use a fresh slice of lime each time.

# FRESH TEQUILA
## *Tequila Fresca*

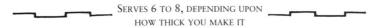 SERVES 6 TO 8, DEPENDING UPON HOW THICK YOU MAKE IT

Clear glass jugs of colorful liquids line the counters of Mexican markets and cafes. Known as *aguas frescas,* or "fresh waters," they are flavorful, colorful, and refreshing drinks blended from fresh fruit, water, and sugar. Here we call for watermelon, but experiment with other fruits such as pineapple, strawberries, or tamarind.

We've added some tequila to the *agua fresca* for a lively, refreshing, and rosy summertime beverage. Don't add too much sugar; the drink should just be a little sweet and this will depend on how sweet the fruit is.

*½ dead-ripe watermelon*
*sugar*
*ice cubes*
*silver tequila as needed*

Cut the watermelon pulp from the rind and seed it. Cut the pulp into chunks and place in a blender. Purée until smooth. Pour the purée through a sieve into a pitcher. Add sugar to taste and dilute with water to desired consistency. Cover and refrigerate until very cold.

Pour the watermelon water over ice in a glass. Add a jigger or so of tequila, stir well, and serve.

### TEQUILA BEETLES

Surely one of the strangest promotions ever devised was a stunt in the 1960s sponsored by Schenley Olé Tequila. Schenley offered to paint Olé Tequila adverts all over Volkswagen Beetles, and apparently thousands of car owners took him up on the offer.

### BARTENDER, THERE'S A WORM IN MY DRINK!

If it has a worm in it, it isn't tequila. It's mescal. The little beast is put there as a kind of guarantee that it is really mescal in the bottle, since the worm is a pest on the agave plant. Worms are never put in tequila, which from the standpoint of a confirmed tequila drinker is a very good thing.

### CAFÉ OLLA

Back on the dusty rancheros in Mexico's deep country-side, they brew a coffee called *café olla* that is strong enough to make anyone sit up and take notice. It's simple to make—just add one tablespoon of coffee plus one for the pot for each cup of boiling water in a clay or enamel pot. Let it boil for four or five minutes, then add sugar and ground cinnamon to taste. A few splashes of tequila does it no harm at all.

# Antojitos

Mexicans love to nibble. But don't we all. A bit of
this and maybe a little taste of that, and how about
a mouthful of that over there? Perhaps they picked
up the habit from the Spanish, who have made tapas
something of an institution. But the Mexicans have
also taken snacking to the street. Walk down any
sidewalk or around any tree-shaded plaza in Mexico
and you will be tempted by the aromas of food being
cooked on the spot by street vendors, who oversee
everything from utterly simple tamale carts to elaborate stands outfitted with butane or wood-burning
stoves.

Every marketplace has aisles filled with food
stands, many offering irresistible little treats to
tempt the palate while the shopper makes serious
decisions about what will go in the dinner pot. In
fact, the food in the market is often so tasty it is a
wonder dinner ever gets prepared.

We love these little bites—*antojito* means a
little *antojo,* or "sudden desire," so *antojito* could
be translated as a sudden urge to eat a small something—and we have included recipes for many of
our favorites. But beyond that these foods, often on
the spicy side, go very well with a small glass of
chilled tequila.

# Shark Bites, or The Surfer's Revenge
## *Venganza del Pescador*

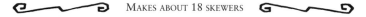 Makes about 18 skewers

We serve these as appetizers, so we only put one piece of shark on each skewer, but for a lunch or dinner course you could slide on two or three. We first had these at the home of a Mexican fisherman, who said the dish came from the days when no one would buy shark meat in the market, so the fishermen ate it themselves.

> *1 pound shark fillet*
> *2 tablespoons Here's the Rub (see page 106)*
> *2 tablespoons fresh lime juice*
> *½ teaspoon salt*

You will need about 18 small metal or bamboo skewers. If using bamboo skewers, soak them in water to cover for 1 hour.

Rub your fingers over the shark fillet, removing any bones you feel. Cut the fish into roughly 2-inch cubes. You should have about 18 cubes. In a small bowl, mix together the rub, juice, and salt. Using your fingers, rub the marinade into the shark. Thread the shark cubes onto the skewers and place on a baking sheet. Let stand for 30 minutes at room temperature.

Meanwhile, preheat a broiler. Broil the fish, turning once, until opaque when pierced, a few minutes on each side. Serve immediately.

# ROOSTER'S BITE
## *Pico de Gallo*

 SERVES 6

*Pico de gallo* is as sharp as a peck from a rooster's beak. And that's exactly the sensation this powdered mixture imparts to fruit. When I first saw this chili salt sprinkled over fruits in the ranchero kitchen of an old friend in Jalisco, I thought it was a shame to mask the flavors of freshly picked fruits. But after I tasted it, it brought back memories of growing up in the Midwest, where we put salt on our watermelon and ground black pepper on our cantaloupe. The spices actually intensify the fruit flavors.

An alternative to sprinkling the tequila over the fruit is to serve it on the side in a chilled tumbler. *Pico de gallo* gets the taste buds up and running, so it makes a great appetizer.

> 2½ *pounds mixed ripe, seasonal fruits such as oranges,*
>   *melons, grapefruits, mangoes, and papayas, peeled,*
>   *seeded, and cut into serving-sized pieces*
> 2 *tablespoons powdered* ancho *chili*
> 1 *teaspoon salt*
> 1 *teaspoon freshly ground black pepper*
> ½ *teaspoon cayenne pepper*
> 2 *teaspoons paprika*
> 2 *tablespoons fresh lime juice, mixed with 2 tablespoons*
>   *silver tequila*

Arrange the fruits on a platter. Combine the chili, salt, black and cayenne peppers, and paprika in a small bowl. Stir well and nest the bowl in the center of the fruits.

Sprinkle the lime-tequila mixture over the fruits. Each person sprinkles chili mixture on the fruits to his or her taste.

# STUFFED ROLLS IN A BATH
*Bolitas en un Baño*

 SERVES 6

These are both the messiest and the most delicious sandwiches. They are taking a "bath" in the sauce, and you will probably need a bath, too, when you finish eating one. But it's worth it!

*½ onion, chopped*
*4 large cloves garlic, chopped, plus 2 medium cloves garlic*
*2 pork tenderloins, 1 pound each*
*2 tablespoons corn oil*
*6 fresh* árbol *chilies*
*½ teaspoon dried oregano*
*3 whole cloves*
*1 cinnamon stick*
*1 tablespoon distilled white vinegar*
*¼ cup tequila*
*salt*
*freshly ground black pepper*
*6 crusty rolls, split in half lengthwise*

In a saucepan combine the onion, chopped garlic, whole tenderloins, and enough water to cover. Bring to a boil, reduce the heat to medium, and simmer, uncovered, until tender, about 20 minutes.

Drain, reserving the liquid. Set the pork and the onions and the garlic aside separately. Measure the cooking liquid and add water as needed to measure 1½ cups. Set the liquid aside.

Using your fingers, shred the pork. In a skillet over medium-high heat, warm the corn oil. Add the shredded pork and the reserved onion and garlic and fry, stirring, until browned, about 5 minutes. Remove from the heat and set aside; cover to keep warm.

In a saucepan combine the chilies, oregano, cloves, cinnamon stick, the 2 medium garlic cloves, vinegar, and the reserved cooking liquid. Bring to a boil, reduce the heat to medium, and cook for 20 minutes. Remove the cinnamon stick and the stems from the chilies and discard. Transfer the contents of the saucepan to a blender and blend until smooth. Stir in the tequila and season to taste with salt and pepper.

Stuff the rolls with fried meat. Put each stuffed roll in a shallow soup bowl. Pour the hot sauce evenly over the rolls. Allow the rolls to rest in the sauce and absorb it for about 5 minutes.

Serve the rolls hot with big napkins, knives, and forks.

# TEQUILA-MARINATED
# SEAFOOD COCKTAIL
*Vuelve a la Vida*

 SERVES 6

The name translates idiomatically as "return to life." This great hangover helper first came to our rescue at the Bar Andaluz, next to the vast Mercado Libertad in Guadalajara. The seafood comes fresh from the market, where virgin versions of the cocktail are sold. The tequila adds a real punch, but also deepens and enriches the taste of the seafood.

In Jalisco's markets these cocktails are often served in the kind of glasses found in old-fashioned soda fountains. Use something a little whimsical to present your cocktails.

> *1 vine-ripened tomato, finely diced*
> *½ cup cilantro leaves (from about ½ small bunch), finely chopped*
> *2 green onions, minced, including some of the green tops*
> *2 fresh serrano chilies, stemmed, seeded, and diced*
> *1 cup water*
> *6 oysters in the shell, scrubbed (fresh is best but use canned shucked oysters if you must)*
> *6 mussels in the shell, scrubbed and debearded*
> *18 medium-large shrimp in the shell (about 1 pound)*
> *1½ cups cooked crab meat (about ¾ pound), picked over for shell fragments*
> *¼ cup silver tequila*
> *1 lemon, cut lengthwise into 6 slices*

Combine the tomato, cilantro, onions, and chilies in a glass or stainless-steel bowl. Toss gently to mix and set aside.

Put the water in the bottom of a steamer and put the oysters and mussels in the steamer rack over the water. Cover and cook over high heat to steam open the shellfish. Peek under the lid often and remove the shellfish as they open. Discard any that do not open. (If using shucked oysters, remove them as they are cooked.) Set the shellfish aside until cool enough to handle. Do not turn off the heat under the steamer.

Remove the steamer rack from the pot and add the shrimp to the boiling water. Cook until they turn pink, 1 to 2 minutes. Remove the shrimp, reserving the liquid in the pot, and set aside.

Remove the oysters and mussels from their shells, pouring any liquid from the shells into the steamer. Place the oysters and mussels in a bowl. Peel and devein the shrimp and add to the bowl, and then add the crab meat.

Cook the steaming liquid over high heat until reduced to ½ cup. Taste to make sure it is not too salty. If it is, dilute with a small amount of water, to no more than 1 cup. Add the tequila and allow to cool to room temperature.

Toss the shellfish with the cooled liquid. Fold in the tomato mixture and arrange in serving glasses or dishes. Garnish each serving with a slice of lemon and serve immediately.

# DRUNKEN SHRIMP
## Camarónes Borrachos

 SERVES 6

You run into variations on this dish all along the coast of Jalisco. We've even had it served from a *comal* on the beach. It can work as an *antojito* before the meal or as a first course. Either way, it's delicious. The Worcestershire sauce (which both Mexican and Spanish cooks have taken to with great gusto) and tequila together make an especially intriguing blend.

*24 large shrimp (about 2 pounds), peeled and de-veined*
*2 tablespoons silver tequila*
*1 tablespoon olive oil*
*1 tablespoon Worcestershire sauce*
*3 cloves garlic*
*1 teaspoon crumbled dried oregano*
*1 teaspoon salt*
*1 tablespoon paprika*
*1 fresh serrano chili, stemmed and seeded*
*½ cup cilantro leaves (from about ½ small bunch)*

Put the shrimp in a nonreactive bowl. Combine all the other ingredients in a blender and purée until smooth. Pour over the shrimp. Toss with a spoon or use your hands to coat the shrimp well with the marinade. Cover and refrigerate for about 1 hour.

Heat a large nonreactive skillet over high heat until very hot. Add the shrimp and the marinade and cook, tossing, until the shrimp all turn bright pink and are cooked through, 1 to 2 minutes.

Remove to a large platter and serve immediately.

# CHILIES WITH CHEESE
*Chiles con Queso*

This flavorful dip is traditionally made with a dry cheese, but cream cheese gives it a particularly smooth texture. Serve with fresh tortilla chips and a tequila cocktail for a lively summer evening treat.

> *1 tablespoon olive oil*
> *1 onion, minced*
> *3 large, ripe tomatoes, peeled, seeded and puréed until smooth*
> 2 chipotle *chilies canned in red adobo sauce, chopped*
> *¾ pound good-quality cream cheese, cut into small pieces*
> *salt*
> *tortilla chips*

In a heavy-bottom sauce pan over medium heat, warm the olive oil. Add the onion and sauté until soft and beginning to color, about 10 minutes. Add the puréed tomato and the chilies and cook, stirring occasionally, until a thick paste forms, about 5 minutes.

Stir in the cheese and continue to cook and stir until the cheese melts and combines with the tomato sauce, about 2 minutes. Taste for salt and add as needed.

Serve the dip hot, preferably in a chafing dish over a flame. Have a basket of tortilla chips ready for guests to use for scooping up the dip.

# STREET CORNER
# CORN ON THE COB
*Elote con Crema, Salsa Roja con Tequila y Queso*

 SERVES 6

Here is a wonderful picnic or backyard barbecue treat. Just cook the corn in a steamer or pasta cooker right over the charcoal grill. The salsa adds a delectable bite to this classic snack that is as popular on the streets of towns in Michoacán and Jalisco as the walkaway crab cocktail is at San Francisco's Fisherman's Wharf.

> *6 very fresh ears white or yellow corn, shucked and*
>    *cleaned of the silk*
> *1 recipe Mexican Cream (see page 107)*
> *½ recipe Tequila Salsa (see page 105)*
> *1 cup grated dry jack or Asiago cheese*

Cut each ear of corn in half crosswise. Pour water into the bottom of a steamer or pasta cooker and bring to a boil. Arrange the corn on the rack, place over the water, cover, and steam until tender, about 10 minutes.

Place the cream, salsa, and cheese in separate bowls. Spear the cobs onto thickish wooden skewers and place on a platter. Serve with the accompaniments for guests to apply as they wish.

The village of Patzcuaro, on the hillside above Lake Patzcuaro in Michoacán, has managed to avoid the worst excesses of international jet-setters. Perhaps the village has been spared because it is several hours from the nearest major airport, or perhaps it is simply the quiet dignity of the people that has protected it. Whatever the reason, Patzcuaro has managed to maintain a feeling of Mexico "the way it used to be."

There is some very good food to be found in the village, including the tasty fried white fish from the lake. But few things could be more tummy-friendly than a snack of Mexican-style corn on the cob basted with cream, dribbled with hot sauce, then sprinkled with grated cheese, which can be found hot from a boiling pot on almost every street corner around the market square.

# EMPANADILLAS WITH CHEESE, CORN, AND CUMIN
## Empanadillas de Queso y Elote con Comino

Known variously as *empanadas, empanadillas, pasteles,* or *tortas,* these pastries are a cousin to pot pies and a distant relative of the pizza. They can be made with either risen dough, quick dough, or puff pastry and can be stuffed with just about anything you'd like to add. They are found everywhere in the Spanish-speaking world. This version is from Guadalajara and is often served there with a salsa similar to our Tequila Salsa. The *empanadillas* may be frozen for up to six months before cooking and baked directly from the freezer.

FOR THE DOUGH:
*1 cup (½ pound) unsalted butter, at room temperature*
*½ pound cream cheese, at room temperature*
*1 cup fine- or medium-grind cornmeal*
*2 cups all-purpose flour*
*1 teaspoon salt*
*dash of cayenne pepper*

FOR THE FILLING:
*2 teaspoons cumin seeds*
*2 cups fresh or thawed, frozen corn kernels, blanched*
  *2 minutes and drained*
*1½ cups grated good-quality Swiss cheese*
*4 green onions, minced, including some of the green tops*
*1 bunch cilantro, stemmed and leaves minced*
*salt*
*freshly ground black pepper*
*1 recipe Tequila Salsa (optional, see page 105)*

**42**

To make the dough, cut the butter and cream cheese into small chunks and put into a food processor. Add the cornmeal, flour, salt, and cayenne and pulse to form a smooth ball of dough. You will probably need to turn the dough out onto a lightly floured table top and knead by hand to achieve the right consistency.

Preheat an oven to 375°F.

Lightly flour a smooth work surface. Divide the dough into quarters. Roll out 1 portion into a circle about ¾ inch thick. Using a round cutter about 4 inches in diameter, cut out 6 dough rounds. Set rounds aside and cover them with a cloth or a piece of plastic wrap. Repeat with the remaining 3 portions.

To make the filling, toast the cumin seeds in a small, dry, hot skillet over medium heat until they "dance." Remove to a bowl. Add all the remaining filling ingredients, including salt and pepper to taste, and stir to mix well.

Top each dough round with an equal amount of the filling. Fold in half and press the edges together to seal. Then, holding the *empanadilla* in one hand, pat the sealed edges with the palm of the other hand to make a smooth, rounded edge. Arrange the filled *empandillas* 1 inch apart on a baking sheet.

Bake until golden and crisp, about 20 minutes. Serve at once, or allow to cool and serve at room temperature. Offer the salsa on the side.

# BEAN AND CORN TORTILLAS
## *Totopos*

 MAKES 25 TOTOPOS

These *totopos*—a specialty of Michoacán—are even more delicious served with margaritas. Hey, but what isn't? Serve them as is as accompaniments to a stew, or top them with a spoonful of guacamole and a dollop of sour cream and serve as appetizers.

*2 dried* ancho *chilies*
*boiling water as needed*
*½ cup drained, cooked red or pinto beans*
*1½ cups fresh corn* masa *(see* NOTE *next page)*
*1 teaspoon salt*
*corn oil for frying*

Put the chilies in a bowl and add boiling water to cover. Set aside for 15 minutes. Drain the chilies, then stem and seed them. Put into a food processor. Add the beans to the food processor and whirl until smooth. Add the *masa* and salt and whirl again until smooth.

Place a griddle or heavy skillet over medium heat. Scoop out 1 tablespoon dough and roll it lightly between your palms into a ball. Transfer the ball of dough to the fingers of one hand, palm side up, and "pat" into a 3-inch round *totopo* by passing the dough from hand to hand, inverting first one hand then the other over the opposite hand. Keep the dough on the fingers not the palms. Never squish the dough between your hands; it will stick and you will need to start over.

As the *totopos* are formed, put them on the griddle and cook, turning once, about 1 minute on each side until they become firm. Repeat until all dough has been used. Several *totopos* can be cooked simultaneously. The preparation can stop here to be finished later; they should sit no longer than 1 hour.

To serve, place a skillet over medium heat. Add oil to cover the bottom of the skillet. When the oil is hot, working in batches, add the *totopos* and fry, turning once, until crisp, about 1 minute on each side. Drain on paper towels briefly. Serve at once.

NOTE: Fresh corn *masa*, the dough used for making tortillas and tamales, is now widely available in the United States, at stores specializing in Mexican foods and in supermarkets catering to large Hispanic populations. If no fresh *masa* is available in your area, look for Quaker Brand *masa harina* ("dough flour") to make your own. For this recipe, stir together 1¼ cups *masa harina* and ⅔ cup water; use immediately.

# Chilies Stuffed with Corn and Cheese in Cream Sauce

*Pimentos Rellenos con Elote y Queso en Salsa Crema*

 Serves 6

This is a variation on the corn-chili-cheese theme, a common combination in Mexican cookery (see Street Corner Corn on the Cob on page 40). Beautiful and flavorful as a first course or with a salad for lunch or a light supper, this simple street fare makes a good impression at the table. A small glass of *añejo* tequila for sipping matches well with the flavors of this dish.

> 6 *fresh* poblano *chilies*
> 3 *tablespoons corn oil*
> 2 *onions, finely minced*
> 3 *cloves garlic, finely minced*
> *kernels from 4 ears white or yellow corn (about 1½ cups)*
> 2 *cups grated dry or soft jack cheese*
> 1 *teaspoon salt*
> ½ *teaspoon freshly ground black pepper*
> 1 *red bell pepper, stemmed, seeded, and cut into matchstick slivers*
> 1 *recipe Mexican Cream (see page 107)*

Place the chilies on a rack directly over the flame of a gas stove or on a pan under a preheated broiler. Watching carefully, char and blister the skins of the chilies on all sides, turning them so they do not burn and so they color evenly. Transfer to a covered bowl or closed paper bag and let stand for about

20 minutes to "sweat" the chilies. Using your fingertips, peel off the charred skins. Make a lengthwise slit in each chili, remove seeds, and set aside.

Preheat an oven to 400°F.

Heat 2 tablespoons of the oil in a skillet over high heat. Add half of the minced onions and two-thirds of the minced garlic and saute until soft, about 5 to 10 minutes. Transfer to a bowl.

Add the corn and 1½ cups of the cheese to the bowl. Season with ½ teaspoon of the salt and ¼ teaspoon of the black pepper. Stir to mix well. Stuff the chili peppers with the corn mixture. Lay the stuffed peppers in a single layer in glass or clay baking dish.

In a skillet over low heat, warm the remaining 1 tablespoon oil. Add the remaining onion and garlic and sauté over low heat until golden, about 10 minutes. Add the bell pepper slivers and sauté until they soften, another 5 minutes. Stir in the cream and the remaining ½ teaspoon salt and ¼ teaspoon black pepper.

Pour the cream mixture over the peppers in the baking dish and sprinkle with the remaining ½ cup cheese. Place in the oven and bake until pale golden brown, about 30 minutes. Serve at once directly from the baking dish.

Francisco Fernandez has been a *jimador* for thirty-five years. He started work with his father in the agave fields when he was twelve years old. For a few years, his son worked beside him, but his son left the *campo* ten years ago and works in a hotel in Guadalajara. "It was too hard for him here," Francisco explained. "I don't blame him for leaving. He has an apartment in the city. His wife has a good job in an office, and there is plenty of money for the children, for clothes, for school. There is not much here for anyone." As he spoke, Francisco looked around the yard of the small, whitewashed concrete block house, one of several dozen clustered around a distillery on the outskirts of Tequila. There were several chickens scrabbling around the packed dirt yard, out looking for the early worm in the first gray light of dawn.

We squeezed into Francisco's battered pickup, and the rest of the crew climbed into the back. Each man carried his own *coa,* a long pole the length of a garden rake, with a narrow iron blade for cutting away the tough leaves surrounding the *piña* and then freeing it from its roots.

That day, we were in the field before the sun had risen. As the foreman of this work crew, Francisco knew which plants were ready to harvest. No one rushed. A hurried blow from the *coa* could damage a *piña,* releasing some of the precious *miel.* On a good day, a single *jimador* can harvest well over a ton of *piñas.* Once the giant bulbs are free of the ground, they are left for other workers to carry back to a pickup truck that sits at the end of the row. By noon, or before, there would be a truck loaded with *piñas* ready to return to the distillery.

# ANITA'S VEGETARIAN TAMALES
## Tamales de Verduras de Anita

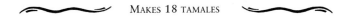 MAKES 18 TAMALES

Vegetarian tamales are hardly a regular menu item in Mexico, but Anita Torres, a good friend and superb cook, developed this recipe for our California catering business, basing it on her family recipe for tamales. When buying the *masa*, ask for *masa* without lard for tamales. If it is impossible to find this *masa* in your area, use the *masa* for tortillas. This will not have any fat added, but will have a different texture than *masa* made for tamales. Corn husks can be bought at most Mexican markets and many supermarkets in areas with sizable Hispanic populations. These tamales make a great snack served with a margarita. Once cooked, they may be frozen for up to six months.

*clean, dry corn husks to make 18 tamales (1 to 2 pounds)*

FOR THE FILLING:
*6 dried* guajillo *chilies*
*6 dried* ancho *chilies*
*boiling water as needed*
*1 tablespoon corn oil*
*⅔ cup fresh or thawed, frozen corn kernels*
*½ cup diced zucchini (¼ inch)*
*½ cup diced, peeled carrots (¼ inch)*
*salt*

FOR THE DOUGH:
*3 pounds fresh corn* masa *if available (see* NOTE *on page 51)*
*1 pound butter, melted and cooled*
*1½ teaspoons baking powder*
*1 teaspoon salt*

Carefully go over the corn husks, removing any corn silk. Cover the husks with hot water and let stand for 1 hour. Drain the husks and squeeze dry. Separate out the largest husks to be filled; set aside the smaller husks.

To make the filling, put the chilies in a bowl and add boiling water to cover. Set aside for 15 minutes. Drain the chilies, reserving the liquid. Stem and seed the chilies and place in a blender. Add a little of the soaking liquid and purée until smooth. Add more of the liquid as needed to make a medium-thick sauce. Pour the sauce through a sieve to remove any remaining seeds.

Heat the oil in a large skillet over medium heat. Add the corn kernels, zucchini, and carrots and cook, stirring for 5 minutes. Add the sauce and continue to cook over medium heat until the vegetables are soft, about 10 minutes. Remove from the heat, season to taste with salt, and set aside to cool.

To make the dough, put the *masa* in a large bowl. Pour the butter over the *masa* and sprinkle on the baking powder and salt. Using your hands, work the dough to distribute the ingredients evenly.

To assemble the tamales, hold 1 wide husk (or if the husks are not wide enough, overlap 2 or 3 husks) in your palm, or place flat on a work surface. Have the pointed end of the husk at the top. Smear about 2 tablespoons of the dough in the center at the widest part of the husk, but not up to any of the edges. Place a heaping tablespoon of the filling on the center of the dough. Bring up the top and bottom edges of the husk until they meet, pressing the dough together to seal the tamales at the sides. Set the tamale aside while you prepare the remaining tamales in the same manner.

Pour water into the bottom of a steamer. Put the steamer rack in place and arrange a layer of the small husks on the rack. Set the prepared tamales upright atop the husks, folded edge down.

Cover the tamales with another layer of the small corn husks. Cover the steamer tightly and bring the water to a boil. Reduce the heat and cook at a slow boil until the tamales are cooked, about 40 minutes.

The tamales taste great fresh from the steamer, but they can be reheated in the steamer. Or wrap a few at a time in a plastic bag or in a dampened paper towel and heat in the microwave for 1 minute.

NOTE: If fresh corn *masa* is not available, stir together 7 cups *masa harina* and 4 cups water. See note on page 45 for information on fresh *masa* and *masa harina*.

# Soups & Salads

The Goddess of Soup—*La Nuestra Señora de la Sopa*—
has made her home in Mexico for centuries. Mexicans
take their soup seriously and most midday meals
feature some sort of soup. There are soups that include
every ingredient imaginable, from avocado to pumpkin
seeds, and a dash of tequila can enliven almost any of
them, too.

Of course, the heart of a good soup is a good
stock. Stocks are not difficult to make and are easy
to keep on hand, so we've included a good basic
chicken stock, which will help you bring your soup
up to Mexican standards.

Mexican meals often open with a simple green
salad, but Mexican cooks can also be very inventive
at the salad bowl. Fruit is frequently the basis for
a delicious salad and some salads can be meals in
themselves.

# CHICKEN STOCK
## *Caldo de Pollo*

It is much more economical to buy a whole chicken rather than chicken parts. Not only do you save money, but with the whole bird you have all those backs and wing tips for stock. Just put the extra parts in a plastic bag and freeze them until you have enough to make a good stock. You can even freeze the cooked chicken carcass for stock.

Once you have prepared the stock, cover and refrigerate it. When the fat solidifies on top, take it off; pour the stock into small containers or ice cube trays and freeze for use later. It will keep frozen for up to six months. If you freeze it in ice trays, empty the trays into plastic bags, close tightly, and slip the bags into the freezer. You can easily remove as much as you want. The yield will vary, depending upon how much you reduce the stock and how much chicken you start with.

When making stock, keep in mind that you do not have to have exactly the "right" ingredients on hand. We have often thrown in half of a head of lettuce or a potato, for example.

> *about 5 pounds chicken wings, backs, and the like*
> *1 or 2 onions*
> *1 or 2 carrots*
> *1 or 2 bay leaves*
> *1 celery stalk, if you have one*

Put the chicken parts in a large stockpot and add cold water to cover by a couple of inches. Add the onions, carrots, and bay leaves—the number depends upon the amount of bones—and

**54**

a stalk of celery if one is at hand. Bring to a boil and skim off the foam that rises to the top. Reduce the heat to very low and cook for about 2 hours. A covered stock will cook longer and will yield an even more intense stock.

Strain the stock into a bowl. Discard the bones and vegetables. When the stock is cool, cover and refrigerate it until the fat congeals on top. At this point you can remove the fat and boil the stock uncovered to reduce it and intensify the flavor.

# AVOCADO-TEQUILA CREAM SOUP
*Sopa de Crema de Aguacate con Tequila*

 SERVES 4 TO 6

Here is a marvelously cooling soup for a hot summer's day lunch. We found this recipe on the coast on just such a day and liked it so much we went back to the cafe in mid-afternoon for another small bowl.

> *2 very ripe avocados, peeled and pitted*
> *1½ cups plain nonfat yogurt*
> *1½ cups chilled, good-quality chicken stock, preferably*
> *homemade (see page 54)*
> *1 or 2 dashes Tabasco sauce*
> *1 teaspoon salt*
> *2 tablespoons silver tequila*
> *½ recipe Fresh Tomato Salsa (see page 102)*

Put the avocados in a blender. Add the yogurt, stock, Tabasco, salt, and tequila and purée. Pour into a bowl, cover, and chill for 1 hour. Taste for seasoning.

To serve, divide the chilled soup among 4 to 6 soup bowls. Put a dollop of salsa in the center of each bowl and serve immediately.

# TEQUILA-LIME
# SHELLFISH SOUP
*Sopa de Mariscos con Límon Verde al Vapor de Tequila*

 SERVES 6

This soup from the coast of Jalisco can be made hotter by adding more chilies. Don't be afraid to play around a bit with the ingredients, too; the number of shellfish is flexible, depending upon what is available and whether you want the soup to start the meal or be the meal.

> *1 large bunch cilantro, plus 6 cilantro sprigs for garnish*
> *2 fresh serrano chilies, seeded, stemmed, and sliced into*
> *rounds*
> *3 cloves garlic, smashed*
> *½ onion, sliced*
> *1 tomato, cut in half*
> *2½ quarts water*
> *12 mussels in the shell, scrubbed and debearded*
> *12 clams in the shell, scrubbed*
> *2 large shrimp, peeled and de-veined*
> *2 tablespoons silver tequila*
> *juice of 2 limes*
> *salt*
> *6 avocado slices*

Tie the cilantro bunch, chilies, garlic, onion, and tomato in a piece of cheesecloth. Put the cheesecloth bag in a large pot and add the water. Bring to a boil, reduce the heat to medium, and simmer, uncovered, for 30 minutes. Remove the bag, squeeze any juice from it back into the pot, and discard the bag.

Return the broth to a boil and boil until reduced by half. Add the mussels and, as they open, remove them to a platter. (Discard any that do not open.) Repeat with the clams. Add the shrimp and cook until they turn pink, about 1 minute; remove from the broth.

Strain the broth into another pot to remove any sand or grit. Bring the broth to a boil and reduce the heat to a simmer. Add the tequila and lime juice. Taste for salt and add as desired.

Distribute the shellfish evenly among 6 bowls. Ladle the broth over the shellfish. Garnish each bowl with a slice of avocado and a sprig of cilantro. Serve immediately.

Chilies, which are native to Mexico, come in a truly bewildering variety of shapes, sizes, and colors, and the naming of them is a work in progress. The same chili is called one thing here, quite another thing there.

Entire books have been written about chilies. In this book, we have confined ourselves to the following:

*Ancho,* a dried, reddish-brown chili, is one of the most common Mexican chiles. About 5 inches or slightly longer and 2 to 3 inches wide, *ancho* is the dried form of the *poblano,* a fresh, usually rather mild chili. Demonstrating the confusion over the names of chilies, the *ancho* is sometimes called *pasilla* in California, even though the *pasilla* is actually the dried *chilaca.* The *ancho* can be found in powdered form in many Mexican markets.

*Árbol* is a dried chili 2 to 3 inches long, narrow, bright red, and quite fiery

*Chipotle* is a brownish chili, a bit over 2 inches long and $^1\!/_2$ to $^3\!/_4$ inch wide. It is the dried, smoked version of the *jalapeño* chili, a fairly hot pepper that is readily found fresh and is also available canned in *escabeche,* essentially pickled. *Chipotles* are themselves canned in an *adobo* sauce, a paste made of spices, chilies, herbs, and vinegar.

*Guajillo* is a dried chili. It is a pointed, slim pepper with reddish-ochre skin, 4 to 5 inches long, and 1 to $1^1\!/_2$ inches wide. It is sometimes mistakenly called *cascabel;* a smaller version is called *pulla.* The *guajillo* packs a lot of heat.

*Serrano* is a fresh green chili, about $1^1\!/_2$ inches long and $^1\!/_2$ inch wide. It is round or slightly pointed at one end.

When working with chilies take care not to rub your eyes after seeding and de-veining them, as the seeds and veins are the really fiery parts. Wear rubber gloves or be careful to clean your hands and fingers thoroughly after handling the chilies.

# Fresh Corn Soup with Tomatoes, Lime, and Tequila

*Sopa de Elote con Tomate y Límon Verde*

 Serves 6

A perfect starter to a complex or heavier meal. The flavors are light and clean and rely on corn at the height of the season. And the dash of tequila enhances the flavor of the corn.

> *6 cups chicken stock, preferably homemade (see page 54)*
> *salt*
> *white pepper*
> *kernels from 3 ears white or yellow corn (about 1 cup)*
> *3 tomatoes, peeled, seeded, and diced*
> *juice of 1½ limes*
> *leaves from 1 bunch cilantro*
> *silver tequila*

In a large pot bring the stock to a boil. Season to taste with salt and white pepper. Add the corn and cook until just tender, about 5 minutes. Add the tomatoes and cook until heated through, about 30 seconds. Stir in the lime juice and half of the cilantro leaves.

Ladle the soup into 6 individual bowls. Sprinkle the tops with the remaining cilantro leaves. Add a dash of tequila to each bowl and serve immediately.

# CARMELA'S FRUIT SALAD
## *Ensalada de frutas de Carmela*

 SERVES 6

We were first served this refreshing salad in the cool, inviting patio of Carmen Guttierrez, at her family's home in Morelia. A pitcher of margaritas stood near at hand. It makes a delightful summer lunch all by itself.

> 2 pink grapefruits
> 1 ripe but firm mango, peeled, pitted, and cubed
> 2 ripe but firm avocados, peeled, pitted, and sliced
>    lengthwise
> 1 ripe but firm papaya, peeled, seeded, and cubed
> ⅓ cup honey
> ¼ cup silver tequila

Peel the grapefruits and remove all the white membrane. Pull the sections apart and remove the seeds. Place the sections in an attractive glass or other nonreactive bowl. Add the mango, avocados, and papaya.

In a small bowl beat together the honey and tequila until well combined. Add to the fruit and toss gently. Cover and refrigerate for at least 1 hour before serving. After several hours the fruit begins to break down so it's better not to keep the compote overnight.

Serve chilled.

# CAESAR SALAD, MEXICAN STYLE
## Ensalada Caesar Mexicana

SERVES 8 TO 10 ON A BUFFET,
OR 6 FOR A LUNCHEON

Here we play fast and loose with a real Mexican recipe. The original Caesar, so one story goes, originated in Tijuana. This version brings the old Caesar back to life. It makes a colorful and delicious buffet salad or can be a luncheon stand-alone.

> *2 heads romaine lettuce*
> *1 large clove garlic*
> *1 teaspoon Dijon-style mustard*
> *5 anchovy fillets, drained*
> *1 tablespoon silver tequila*
> *⅓ cup olive oil*
> *3 tablespoons fresh lime juice*
> *½ teaspoon freshly ground black pepper*
> *salt (optional)*
> *½ recipe Fresh Tomato Salsa (see page 102)*
> *½ cup grated jalapeño jack cheese*
> *2 large handfuls tortilla chips, crushed*

Remove and discard the tough outer leaves and the core of the romaine. Tear the remaining leaves into bite-sized pieces and put into a salad bowl.

To prepare the dressing, put the garlic, mustard, anchovies, and tequila in a blender. Whirl for 1 minute. Combine the oil and lime juice and, with the motor running, gradually add to the blender. Whirl until combined. Add the pepper and taste for seasoning. Add salt if you wish.

Pour the dressing over the romaine and toss well. Use your hands so you can feel when each leaf is well coated. Add the salsa, cheese, and chips and toss well again. Serve on a platter or on individual plates.

# BLACK BEAN, CORN, AND RICE SALAD
### Ensalada de Frijoles Negros, Maiz y Arroz

 SERVES 6 TO 8

Visually lively and full of flavor, this salad can be the main course, or serve it as a side dish at a picnic with Beefsteak Ranchero (see page 97).

*1 pound (2¼ cups) dried black beans*
*2 bay leaves*
*1 tablespoon ground cumin*
*4 teaspoons salt*
*6 ears yellow or white corn, shucked and cleaned of the silk*
*4 green onions, minced, including most of the green tops*
*1 red or green bell pepper, stemmed, seeded, and cut into ¼-inch dice*
*2 cups water*
*1 cup long-grain white rice*
*1 teaspoon cumin seeds*
*½ cup olive oil*
*1 tablespoon red wine vinegar*
*1 teaspoon freshly ground black pepper*
*½ cup minced cilantro leaves*
*½ recipe Tequila Salsa (see page 105)*

Put the black beans in a large pot with the bay leaves and ground cumin. Add water to cover generously. Bring to a boil, reduce the heat to medium-low, and simmer, uncovered, until tender, about 1 hour. Add 1 teaspoon salt and cook for another 10 minutes. Remove from the heat, drain well, and place in a bowl. Let cool to room temperature.

Bring a large pot of water to a boil. Add the corn and 1 teaspoon salt, cover, and remove from the heat. Let rest for 20 minutes. Remove the corn and, when cool enough to handle, cut the kernels from the cobs and place in a bowl. Discard the cobs. Add the onions and bell pepper and toss well with the corn. Set aside.

Bring the 2 cups water to a boil in a saucepan. Add 1 teaspoon salt and the rice and stir. Reduce the heat to low, cover, and cook until done, about 20 minutes. Remove from the heat, uncover, and fluff with a fork. Set aside.

Toast the cumin seeds in a small, dry, hot skillet over medium heat until they "dance."

In a small bowl whisk together the oil, vinegar, the remaining 1 teaspoon salt, and pepper. Stir in the toasted cumin seeds. Toss one third of the dressing with the beans, one third with the corn, and the rest with the rice.

Place the beans on a round platter. Top them with the corn, leaving a 1-inch border of the beans showing. Top the corn with the rice, leaving a 1-inch border of the corn showing. Sprinkle the cilantro leaves over the rice.

Serve immediately with the salsa on the side, or cover and refrigerate and serve chilled.

# FISH

The tequila zone of Mexico is rich in fish and shell-fish from the coast. The interior rivers and lakes of the west-central highlands—Jalisco and Michoacán—yield an equally amazing variety of freshwater fish that must be seen and tasted to be believed.

Some freshwater edibles, especially in the back country where the fishmongers aren't concerned about what the gringos think, look like tiny monsters from the kind of horror films that Joe Bob Briggs reviews. They can be seen at the village market, displayed fin-to-fin with tasty lake white fish, trout, frogs, and turtles. Coastward, market tables are piled with more familiar ocean fish along with mouth-watering displays of shellfish.

The recipes here are little more than an introduction to the marvelous fish of Mexico. Use them to whet your appetite, then go exploring on your own.

Near Lake Patzcuaro is the ancient Tarascan capital of Tzintzuntzán, which means "place of the humming-birds." The ruined stone city stands on a hillside, looking out over the lake and a scattering of villages. The site dates from the late thirteenth or early fourteenth century, and the kings of the Tarascans dominated the area that is now the modern states of Michoacán, Jalisco, and Colima, prime pulque and tequila territory. Some of the ruins have been restored and some haven't yet been uncovered. Work proceeds in fits and starts, depending on the whim of the budget makers in Mexico City. Of the few tourists who make their way to Patzcuaro, most flash past these intriguing ruins, intent on getting a glimpse of the famed butterfly fishing nets that have been used to scoop up the small white fish of the lake for more than one thousand years.

One night in the Posada de la Basilica in Patzcuaro, we ordered a platter of the *pescado blanco,* prepared very much as the Tarascans must have fixed them centuries ago. The fish were fried until just crisp and served with a mild salsa on the side, similar to the Fresh Tomato Salsa on page 102. Each fish made two or three bites. The delicacy of the fish was set off nicely by the smoky fruit of a silver tequila.

# FISH TACOS
## WITH CABBAGE SALSA
*Tacos de Pescado con Salsa de Repollo*

 SERVES 6

Cabbage isn't usually associated with Mexican food, but in fact it is often used, especially in the countryside. We've also had this dish using the small, white, freshwater fish from Lake Patzcuaro.

> *1½ pounds fish fillets, such as snapper or rock cod*
> *½ cup all-purpose flour*
> *½ teaspoon salt*
> *½ teaspoon ground cumin*
> *½ teaspoon freshly ground black pepper*
> *dash of cayenne pepper*
> *2 tablespoons olive, canola, or corn oil*
> *12 corn tortillas*
> *1 recipe Cabbage Salsa (see page 104)*

Preheat an oven to 150°F. Run your fingers over the fish fillets, removing any bones you feel. Cut the fillets into long strips about 1 inch wide. Combine the flour, salt, cumin, and black and cayenne pepper in a shallow dish or pan. Toss the fish with the flour mixture and shake the fish to remove excess flour.

Heat the oil in an 8-inch skillet over high heat. When the oil is hot, add the fish and fry, turning once, until golden on both sides. This should take only a few minutes. Transfer to paper towels to drain. Keep warm in the oven while heating the tortillas.

Heat the tortillas over a gas burner one at a time just until soft; wrap them in aluminum foil to keep them warm. If you have an electric stove, heat the tortillas in a dry skillet, one at a time, until soft and wrap them in foil as well. The warm tortillas will sweat in the foil, making them even softer and accentuating their corn flavor.

Serve the warm tortillas with the fried fish and the salsa for guests to assemble, or put the fish tacos together in the kitchen and serve on a large platter.

### IT IS TOO AUTHENTIC!

When we tested the Fish Tacos with Cabbage Salsa, one of our guinea pigs accused us of making it up, unable to believe that it was actually a Mexican recipe. Not only is it Mexican, we first tasted it on the beach near San Blas, a couple of hundred miles down the road from the village of Tequila. The fish was cooked over an open fire, then rolled in fresh, handmade tortillas with the cabbage salsa. Absolutely simple and simply delicious. Also, the flavor of tequila matches surprisingly well with the flavors of cabbage, as we discovered almost at once. What a treat!

# GRILLED SALMON WITH WARM AVOCADO-TEQUILA SAUCE

*Salmon Parrillado con Salsa Templada de Aguacate y Tequila*

 SERVES 6

An impressive, palate-pleasing dinner dish that can be done without a lot of fuss. We like to serve the salmon steaks with black beans. The flavors are great together and the visual appeal is fabulous.

> 6 salmon steaks, about ½ pound each
> olive oil
> 1 large ripe avocado, peeled and pitted
> 1 large clove garlic
> 2 tablespoons fresh lime juice
> 2 tablespoons silver tequila
> 1 teaspoon salt, plus salt for sprinkling on the salmon
> 1 canned jalapeño chili
> 1 cup fish stock or bottled clam juice

Fire up the charcoal or preheat a broiler. Put the salmon steaks on a platter and drizzle about 1 teaspoon oil over them. Using your hands, work the oil into both sides of the salmon steaks. Set aside.

In a blender combine the avocado, garlic, lime juice, tequila, 1 teaspoon salt, chili, and stock or clam juice. Purée until smooth, then pour into a small, nonreactive saucepan.

Lightly sprinkle the salmon on both sides with salt. Place the salmon steaks on an oiled grill rack over hot coals, or on a broiler pan slipped under a hot broiler. Or you can pan-broil them over medium-high heat. The steaks will take about 5 minutes on each side to cook through.

While the fish is cooking, warm the sauce over low heat until heated through. Do not boil the sauce.

To serve, arrange the steaks on 6 individual plates and divide the sauce among them, spooning it over the top. Serve immediately.

# SNAPPER WITH OLIVES
## Huachinango con Aceitunas

 SERVES 6

A delicate, satisfying dish that can be served as a first or main course. It can be very quickly prepared and there is no added oil, so it's good for you, too! On a hot summer's evening serve the dish cold as a first course.

1 large onion, thinly sliced
2 tomatoes, peeled and thinly sliced
½ cup pimiento-stuffed green olives, chopped
1 teaspoon salt
1 teaspoon freshly ground black pepper
2 pounds snapper fillets
¼ cup silver tequila
¼ cup cilantro leaves

Put half of the onion and tomato slices in a nonreactive 8- or 10-inch skillet. Sprinkle with half of the olives and half of the salt and pepper. Run your fingers over the fish fillets, removing any bones you feel. Place the fish fillets on top of the tomatoes and onions, then cover the fish with the remaining tomatoes, onions, olives, salt, and pepper. Pour the tequila evenly over the fish and scatter the cilantro leaves over the top.

Turn the heat on high under the skillet. Cover the skillet tightly, reduce the heat to medium-low, and cook the fish for 15 to 20 minutes. Check the fish after 15 minutes; if it flakes, remove from the heat.

Arrange the fish on a heated platter with about half of the vegetables and cover to keep warm.

Pour the vegetables and juices remaining in the skillet into a blender. Purée until smooth. Return the purée to the skillet and cook over high heat for about 1 minute until it thickens slightly.

Pour the sauce over the fish and serve immediately.

# SOUSED SNAPPER
## Huachinango en Escabeche

 SERVES 6

*Escabeche* and *ceviche* are often confused. In *escabeche*, the fish, meat, or vegetables are cooked first and then marinated. In *ceviche*, the marinade actually "cooks" the food. *Escabeches* are great for picnics or buffets since they can be left at room temperature safely for a couple of hours. Serve with crusty bread to dip into the juices.

>⅓ cup all-purpose flour
>1 teaspoon salt
>½ teaspoon freshly ground black pepper
>¼ cup plus 2 tablespoons olive oil
>2 pounds snapper fillets
>1 large red onion, thinly sliced
>6 large cloves garlic, sliced
>1 cup rice wine vinegar
>1 cup dry white wine
>2 fresh serrano chilies, stemmed, seeded, and minced
>2 tablespoons silver tequila
>½ cup cilantro leaves (about ½ small bunch)
>½ cup thin radish slices

Run your fingers over the fish fillets, removing any bones you feel. Combine the flour, salt, and pepper in a shallow dish or pan. Heat the ¼ cup oil in a nonreactive skillet over medium heat. Dip the fillets in the flour mixture and shake them to remove excess flour. Add the fish to the hot oil and fry, turning once, until golden on each side. This should take only a few minutes. Remove the fish to paper towels to drain.

Add the remaining 2 tablespoons oil to the same skillet over medium-low heat. Add the onion and garlic and sauté until golden, about 10 minutes. (Watching the color is more important than watching the clock.) Pour in the vinegar and wine and add the chilies. Raise the heat and cook rapidly to reduce by half. Reduce the heat to medium and return the fish to the skillet. Cook, turning the fish several times, until cooked through when pierced with a knife, about 5 minutes. Remove from the heat. Sprinkle the tequila over the fish.

Arrange the contents of the skillet on a nonreactive platter and let cool. Cover and refrigerate for at least 3 hours or for up to 24 hours before serving.

To serve, baste the fish with the collected juices. Garnish with the cilantro and radishes.

There was a crude, hand-lettered sign propped against a trash can beside the road a few miles outside the village of Tequila. The sign, spray-painted on a piece of plywood, said, *"Pulque, aqui."* Two ravens watched us from the roof of the small tin-sided building as we bounced onto the rock and gravel driveway. Inside, three old men stood smoking at one end of the bar, seraped and sombreroed. The dark wood bar was decorated with beautiful inlaid tiles and thousands of cigarette burns. The floor was sand. The old men didn't bother to look around when we came in. They stood stiffly and in a silence that had clearly just descended.

It was touch and go for a moment. It has only been in the last few years that *pulquerias* in the city have allowed women to enter. Perhaps such equal drinking opportunity had not yet reached the countryside.

When we asked for two pulques, the bartender—a boy of perhaps twelve—poured two tall glasses of foaming white liquid from a pitcher that he had dipped into a white plastic bucket. Along with the pulque, the boy served a small plate of smashed strawberries. We each took a sip.

It was, to be honest, fairly vile. There is a sour-sweet finish to pulque that is utterly unlike anything you are likely to have tried before in the way of alcoholic beverages. And yet, you try another sip and this time maybe you don't make a face. It is rough, it is raw, but it does have a presence, an authority that you would expect from a much stronger drink. After the second sip, we stirred in a generous dash of smashed strawberries with a wooden stick. It tasted pretty good that way. With another dash of strawberries, it was even better.

# POULTRY & MEATS

There isn't a Mexican cook from the age of ten up who can't do thirty-nine different things with chicken—all legal and delicious. And she probably has even more recipes for pork. Perhaps this is because the Native Americans hunted a wild pig (there is no indication that it was domesticated), so they were familiar with pork when the Spaniards introduced the European swine. There are also many recipes calling for two animals that were domesticated by the Native Americans, turkey and duck. Turkey, in particular, figures in many *moles.*

You find beef everywhere in Mexico, more often than not in the form of a grilled steak. Mexican beef is usually very flavorful, although not as tender as we have become accustomed to in the United States. That's because most Mexican beef is still taken directly from range to slaughterhouse, rather than penned and force-fed. Such beef is tender but lacks the rich, textured flavor of range-raised beef. Goat, especially kid, is also fairly common; lamb and veal less so.

Of all the meats used in Mexico, tequila has a particular affinity for pork and for the *mole* sauces frequently used with turkey and chicken.

# Chicken in Peanut Sauce
*Pollo en Salsa de Cacahuates*

 Serves 6

Eat your heart out, Colonel Sanders. This finger-licking dish is often served on street corners or in the market, prepared in a *comal* over a wood or charcoal fire. Serve with white rice and plenty of warm tortillas.

> 1 *fryer chicken, about 3½ pounds*
> 1 *teaspoon peanut oil*
> 1 *teaspoon salt, plus salt to taste*
> ½ *teaspoon freshly ground black pepper, plus pepper to taste*
> 4 *cloves garlic, minced*
> ½ *cup minced onion*
> ½ *cup minced cilantro, plus 2 tablespoons minced cilantro for garnish*
> ½ *cup unsalted roasted peanuts, plus ¼ cup chopped peanuts for garnish*
> ½ *cup beer*
> 2 chipotle *chilies canned in red* adobo *sauce*
> ⅓ *cup silver tequila*
> 2 *tomatoes, quartered*

Cut the chicken into 8 serving pieces: 2 thighs, 2 drumsticks, and each half breast cut in half crosswise. Save the backs, neck, and wings for the stockpot.

Heat the oil in a 10-inch skillet over medium heat. Use a metal spatula to spread the oil evenly over the surface of the skillet. When the oil is hot, add the chicken pieces, season them with 1 teaspoon salt and ½ teaspoon pepper, and cook, turning,

**80**

until golden on all sides, 15 to 20 minutes. Remove the chicken pieces to a baking dish or clay *casuela* that can be presented at the table.

Preheat an oven to 375°F.

Pour off all but 1 tablespoon of the fat remaining in the skillet. Reheat the skillet over medium heat. Add the garlic and onion and sauté until soft and golden, about 10 minutes.

Meanwhile, in a blender or food processor, combine the ½ cup cilantro, the ½ cup peanuts, the beer, chilies, tequila, and tomatoes. Purée until smooth. Pour the purée into the skillet holding the cooked onions and garlic and cook, stirring, for 2 minutes. Taste for seasoning and adjust according to your taste, keeping in mind that you are adding the purée to the chicken that has been seasoned with salt and pepper. Pour the sauce over the chicken, put it in the oven, and bake until glossy and golden, about 35 minutes.

Remove from the oven and sprinkle with the remaining ¼ cup peanuts and 2 tablespoons cilantro. Serve immediately directly from the baking dish.

# FRUITED CHICKEN
*Pollo en Salsa de frutas con Chiles Anchos*

SERVES 6 TO 8

Fruity and slightly *picante,* this glorious chicken is one of our party favorites. We like to serve it directly from a clay casserole, so the terra-cotta hues of the sauce match the color of the dish. Accompany with white rice or cumin-scented black beans.

*1 fryer chicken, about 3½ pounds*
*6 cups cold water*
*3 dried ancho chilies*
*boiling water as needed*
*½ cup silver tequila*
*1 large banana, peeled*
*1 large apple, peeled, cored, and coarsely cut*
*4 slices canned pineapple, coarsely cut*
*¼ cup chopped walnuts*
*½ cup chopped onion*
*¼ cup white wine vinegar*
*1 clove garlic*
*½ cup cubed, cooked, and peeled potato*
*salt*
*freshly ground black pepper*

Cut the chicken into 8 serving pieces: 2 thighs, 2 drumsticks, and each half breast cut in half crosswise. Set the pieces aside. Put the back, neck, and wings into a pot and add the 6 cups water. Bring to a boil, reduce the heat to medium-high, and cook for 15 minutes. Strain, reserving the liquid; discard the back and neck and set the wings aside.

Return the reserved liquid to the pot and bring to a boil. Add the reserved chicken pieces, including the wings, and return to a boil. Reduce heat to medium and simmer, uncovered, for 20 minutes. Remove the chicken breasts and put into a baking dish or clay *casuela* that can be presented at the table. Cook the remaining pieces for another 10 minutes.

Remove the chicken pieces from the liquid and add to the breast pieces in the baking dish. Skim the fat from the liquid and reduce the liquid over high heat to 2 cups. Remove from the heat and set aside.

Meanwhile, put the *ancho* chilies in a bowl and add boiling water to cover. Set aside for 15 minutes. Drain the chilies, then stem and seed them.

Preheat an oven to 350°F.

In a blender or food processor, combine the chilies, tequila, banana, apple, pineapple, walnuts, onion, vinegar, garlic, and potato. Add the reduced cooking liquid and purée until smooth.

Place a large, nonstick skillet over medium heat and pour in the purée. Fry for about 3 minutes. Season to taste with salt and pepper.

Pour the sauce over the chicken. Put it in the oven and bake about 20 minutes. Serve immediately directly from the baking dish.

Cinnamon is not native to Mexico, but it is a great favorite in Spain and was brought to the New World very early on. The Native Americans took to it with alacrity, using it in many recipes, including mixing it with dried chocolate and adding it to several *moles*. In fact, cinnamon seems such an integral part of Mexican cuisine that it is tempting to follow Joseph Campbell's speculations that there was trade between Southeast Asia and Mexico centuries before Columbus, trade that would have brought cinnamon to the New World.

# CUMIN CHICKEN
## *Pollo Comino*

 SERVES 6

The flavor of cumin matches well with tequila. In this dish, the combination creates a rich spiciness that lingers on the palate. This is a traditional country recipe from the state of Guanajuato, which borders the tequila zone. Roasted potatoes or grilled polenta makes a good side dish.

> *1 fryer chicken, 3½ to 4 pounds*
> *⅓ cup silver tequila*
> *juice of 1 orange*
> *juice of 1 lemon*
> *1 teaspoon cumin seeds*
> *2 teaspoons olive oil*
> *½ teaspoon salt*

Cut the chicken into 8 serving pieces: 2 thighs, 2 drumsticks, and each half breast cut in half crosswise. Put in a nonreactive pan in a single layer. Save the back, neck, and wings for the stockpot. Using a toothpick or skewer, punch little holes in the skin all over the chicken pieces. In a cup stir together the tequila and citrus juices. Pour evenly over the chicken.

In a small, dry, hot skillet over medium heat, toast the cumin seeds until they "dance." Sprinkle the seeds evenly over the chicken.

Cover the chicken and marinate at room temperature for 1 to 4 hours, turning the chicken occasionally. (If you marinate the chicken longer than 1 or 2 hours, you should refrigerate it.)

Remove the chicken from the marinade and pat dry. Set aside the marinade.

Place a large, nonreactive skillet over medium heat and add the oil. When the oil is hot, add the chicken pieces, season with the salt, and cook, turning, until golden on all sides, 15 to 20 minutes.

Pour in the marinade, reduce the heat, cover, and cook until cooked through and juices run clear, about 30 minutes. Uncover and cook briefly to thicken the cooking juices. The juices should be a dark gold and coat the meat nicely.

Arrange the chicken on a warmed platter and serve immediately.

# TURKEY MOLE
### Mole de Guajolote

 SERVES 6

There are dozens of variations on the theme of *mole* in Mexico, many of them pre-Columbian. This particular version comes from the Guadalajara restaurant of a friend. It's a bit simpler than some of the more elaborate *moles,* but is simply delicious. Especially with a glass or two of a chilled silver tequila. As mentioned elsewhere, the flavor of tequila has a delicious affinity with chocolate.

> *2 whole turkey legs, about 4 pounds total weight*
> *2 onions*
> *1 bay leaf*
> *3 dried ancho chilies*
> *3 dried guajillo chilies*
> *boiling water as needed*
> *2 tablespoons olive oil*
> *½ cup whole almonds*
> *1 corn tortilla*
> *2 cloves garlic, chopped*
> *¼ cup sesame seeds*
> *½ teaspoon aniseeds*
> *½ pound tomatoes, coarsely cut*
> *¼ teaspoon ground cloves*
> *¼ teaspoon ground cinnamon*
> *1 ounce unsweetened chocolate, broken up*
> *1 teaspoon salt*
> *1 teaspoon freshly ground black pepper*

Cut each whole leg at the joint of the leg and thigh. Put the 4 turkey pieces in a pot and cover with cold water. Cut 1 onion in quarters and add to the turkey with the bay leaf. Bring to a boil, reduce the heat to medium, and simmer, uncovered until the turkey is tender, about 1 hour. Remove the turkey from the pot and set aside to cool. Raise the heat under the broth to high and reduce the broth to 2 cups. (All of this can be done the day before and refrigerated.)

Put the *ancho* and *guajillo* chilies in a bowl and add boiling water to cover. Set aside for 15 minutes. Drain the chilies and stem and seed them. Place in a blender.

Heat the oil in a small skillet over high heat. Add the almonds and toast, stirring, until golden and "popping," about 2 minutes, but watch the color, not the clock. Using a slotted spoon, remove the almonds to the blender. In the same oil cook the tortilla, turning once, until crisp, about 1 minute. Remove the tortilla, break it up, and add it to the chilies in the blender.

Chop the remaining onion and add it to the same oil over medium heat along with the garlic. Sauté until soft, about 3 minutes. Pour in the sesame seeds and cook the seeds until golden, 1 to 2 minutes. Pour the contents of the skillet into the blender.

Add the aniseeds, tomatoes, cloves, cinnamon, chocolate, salt, and pepper to the blender. Pour in 1 cup of the reduced turkey stock and blend until very smooth.

Pour the puréed sauce into a skillet over medium heat and heat through. Bone the turkey pieces and discard the bones. Shred the meat and stir into the sauce. Cook, stirring occasionally, until the sauce looks thick, rich, and glossy, about 20 minutes. Taste for seasoning and adjust as necessary.

Serve immediately.

## COMAL

The *comal* is widely used in the western highlands of Mexico as well as many other parts of the country. It is made of either tin or earthenware—tin being much more common—and comes in various sizes, with a loop handle on either side. The center is depressed and the outer edges of the pan slope up at an angle. (Think of an automobile hubcap.) The idea is to do the cooking in the depressed space in the center of the pan, then push the chicken or beef or vegetables (or whatever you are cooking) to the slanted sides. The excess fat drains away and the ingredients stay hot. Tortillas are often cooked on the sides of the *comal* at the same time.

## TAKE IT EASY

"Legend has it that, when pressure from the Nahuatl tribes in the North drove the Toltecs out of Tula, their capital in the present-day state of Hidalgo, starting them on their long migrations to the West and South, a woman invented the "wine of the earth." She punched holes in the *maguey* plant (probably *Agave atrovirens*), drew off the sap, and fermented it, making *pulque.* Other women joined her in this noble work, and they then gave a party for the elders, both men and women. Four cups were served to each person; but the leader of one of the tribes, a man called Cuexteco, drank a fifth cup against all advice, became drunk, and took off all his clothes. In shame he fled with his people to the coastal region known as the Huasteca, on the Gulf of Mexico; to this day the inhabitants are said to be a hard-drinking people."

–Elisabeth Lambert Ortiz, *The Complete Book of Mexican Cooking*

# MEDALLIONS OF PORK
# IN ORANGE SAUCE
*Medallónes de Cerdo en Salsa de Naranja*

SERVES 6

Pork is a mainstay of the Mexican kitchen. Many families in both the countryside and the villages raise their own hogs for butchering. It isn't at all uncommon to see a backyard with one or more pigs being prepared for kitchen duty. The flavors of tequila and pork have a delicious affinity, which is perfectly accented by the use of orange juice and zest in this dish. For a more traditional presentation, omit the bed of greens and serve with white rice and vegetables.

> 1 tablespoon olive oil
> 1 pork tenderloin, about 2 pounds, cut into slices
>   ½ inch thick
> ½ teaspoon salt
> ¼ teaspoon freshly ground black pepper
> 1 onion, minced
> ⅓ cup raisins
> 2 oranges, zest removed and juiced
> ¼ cup silver tequila
> ½ cup chicken stock, preferably homemade (see page 54)
> 2 tablespoons well-drained capers
> mixed salad greens for serving

Heat the oil in a large, nonreactive pan over medium heat. Add the pork, season with the salt and pepper, and brown on both sides, about 3 minutes on each side. Using a slotted spoon, remove the pork and set aside. Add the onion and raisins to the same pan and sauté over medium heat until soft and the raisins are plump, about 3 minutes. Pour in the orange juice, tequila, and stock, and add the capers. Return the pork to the pan and cook over medium heat until it is cooked through, about 5 minutes.

To serve, arrange a bed of greens on each plate. Top each with an equal amount of the pork, and then spoon the sauce evenly over the top. Garnish with the orange zest and serve.

# PORK LOIN IN TEQUILA
## *Lomo de Cerdo con Tequila*

 SERVES 6

Mexican cooks who are interested in their country's culinary history know this is as a pre-Columbian dish. The first mention of it by a European was in a letter written by the marchioness Caledrón de la Barca, wife of the first Spanish ambassador to Mexico after independence. She was served the dish during a visit to an isolated ranch, where she was told that it was an Aztec specialty. Instead of tequila, pulque was used, as it would have been in pre-Columbian, pre-tequila times. We have had the dish made with pulque (which is not available in the United States), but we find that tequila is an excellent substitute. In this dish, we prefer the rounder, more full-bodied flavor of an *añejo* or other gold tequila. This goes especially well with a dish of cumin-scented black beans.

> *6 dried* ancho *chilies*
> *boiling water as needed*
> *1 boneless pork loin, 2½ to 3 pounds*
> *6 cloves garlic*
> *1 onion, cut up*
> *½ cup* añejo *or any gold tequila*
> *½ cup warm water*
> *salt*
> *freshly ground black pepper*

Place the chilies in a bowl and add boiling water to cover. Set aside for 15 minutes.

Meanwhile, heat a dry skillet with high sides over high heat. Add the pork, fat side down, and brown, turning, until all sides are golden, about 5 minutes.

While the pork is browning, drain the chilies and stem and seed them. Place in a blender. Add the garlic, onion, tequila, warm water, and salt and pepper to taste. Purée until smooth.

As soon as the pork is browned, pour the chili mixture over it, reduce the heat to low, and cook covered, until the pork is tender, about 1¾ hour, or until a meat thermometer registers 145°F.

Let the meat rest for 10 minutes before slicing and serving.

# GOAT STEW MARIA LUISA
*Birria Maria Luisa*

 SERVES 6 TO 8

We learned this version of *birria* from an old friend, Maria Luisa Molina, at her rancho in Michoacán in the highlands of west-central Mexico. At the rancho, the dressed goat meat is rubbed with herbs and spices and steamed in a pot sealed with masa, the same corn dough that Maria Luisa uses to make tortillas. After steaming, a sauce of *chiles guajillos* strongly flavored with toasted cumin is poured over the pieces and the dish is finished in the oven. It is served with stacks of steaming corn tortillas fresh from the *comal*. The smoky flavors of a glass of *añejo* tequila in hand give this dish a rich, extra depth. If you have trouble locating goat, use six pounds of lamb shanks instead.

> *1 dressed baby goat, about 15 pounds, cut into serving pieces*
> *3 whole cloves*
> *3 whole allspice*
> *2 bay leaves, center spines removed*
> *2 teaspoons crumbled dried oregano*
> *1 teaspoon cumin seeds*
> *1 tablespoon salt*
> *2 teaspoons black peppercorns*
> *flour and water for making a paste*
>
> FOR THE SAUCE:
> *2 tablespoons lard or olive oil*
> *8 dried guajillo chilies*
> *1 tablespoon cumin seeds*
> *salt*

**94**

Wash the goat pieces and pat dry.

In a mortar with a pestle or in a spice grinder, grind together the cloves, allspice, bay leaves, oregano, cumin, salt, and pepper. Rub the mixture into the meat.

Put the meat on a rack over hot water. You can use a multi-tiered Chinese-type steamer, putting some of the meat into each tier. A pasta cooker or two would work well, too, as would a roasting pan with a turkey rack. The idea is to use a vessel that has a rack for holding the meat above the water and has a lid.

Make a paste of flour and water with the consistency of that gooey white glue that used to get all over your clothes in kindergarten. Arrange the meat on the rack(s), cover the vessel(s), and use the paste to seal together the lid(s) and the cooker(s). Place over medium-low heat and cook for 3 hours. Unseal the pan and test the meat; it should be very tender. If not, reseal and continue to cook until it is tender.

Prepare the chilies for the sauce while the meat is cooking. Heat the lard in a skillet until hot but not smoking. Dip in the chilies, one at a time, for a few seconds only. Remove the chilies from the fat and let cool. Wearing rubber gloves, stem and seed the chilies and put into a pot.

When the meat is ready, preheat an oven to 375°F. Remove the meat to a roasting pan or any pan large enough to hold it. Pour out the cooking juices into a bowl and let rest until the fat comes to the top. Skim off the fat and discard. Measure 1 cup of the liquid and add to the chilies. Place over medium-low heat and simmer for about 10 minutes.

Meanwhile, in a small, dry, hot skillet over medium heat, toast the cumin seeds until they "dance." In a mortar with a pestle, grind them to a thick paste with a little water. Toward the end of the cooking time for the chilies, stir in the cumin paste and add salt to taste. Pour the chili mixture into a blender. Purée until smooth.

Pour the purée over the meat. Put it in the oven and bake for about 30 minutes. Serve hot.

# BEEFSTEAK RANCHERO
*Bifsteck Ranchero*

 SERVES 4 TO 6

This is a popular dish all over the north and west of Mexico, but in Jalisco it becomes even more appealing because of the tequila in the marinade, which gives the meat an intriguing, smoky flavor.

> *2½ pounds sirloin steak, about ½ inch thick*
> *2 tablespoons silver tequila*
> *1 lemon*
> *salt*
> *freshly ground black pepper*
> *1 recipe Tomatillo Salsa (see page 103)*

Put the steaks in a nonreactive pan. Pour the tequila over the steaks, then squeeze half a lemon over them. Let rest at room temperature for 1 hour.

While the steak is marinating, start the charcoal. When the coals are hot and white, spread them out evenly over the grate. Put the grill rack in place. Pat the steaks dry, discard the marinade, and put the steaks on the grill rack. Sprinkle with salt and pepper and grill as desired, turning once.

Remove the steaks to a warmed platter and squeeze the other half of the lemon over them. Serve immediately with the salsa.

# VEAL WITH PRUNES
*Ternera con Ciruelas*

 SERVES 6

Veal dishes are not at all common in Mexico. This one almost surely emigrated from Spain in the not-too-distant past and got mixed up with tequila. A bowl of lentils cooked with lots of onions is an ideal side dish.

*1½ cups pitted prunes*
*½ cup silver tequila*
*2 cups water, boiling*
*1 teaspoon butter*
*1 teaspoon olive oil, or as needed*
*1 large onion, minced*
*¼ cup all-purpose flour*
*1 teaspoon salt*
*½ teaspoon freshly ground black pepper*
*1 teaspoon ground cinnamon*
*2 pounds boneless veal stew meat, cut into 2-inch pieces*

Put the prunes in a bowl. Add the tequila and boiling water and let stand for 30 minutes.

Meanwhile, melt the butter with the 1 teaspoon oil in a large skillet over medium heat. Add the onion and sauté until it is soft and golden, about 5 minutes. Using a slotted spoon, remove the onion and set aside. Do not wash the skillet.

In a plastic bag combine the flour, salt, pepper, and cinnamon. Put the veal pieces in the bag and, holding the bag closed, toss the veal until it is evenly coated with the seasoned flour.

Place the skillet over medium heat and add more oil if pan seems dry. Add the veal pieces and brown on all sides, about 5 minutes.

Drain the prunes, reserving the liquid. Set the prunes aside. Pour the prune liquid into the skillet with the veal. Stir over medium heat, scraping the bottom of the skillet to release any browned bits. Cover, reduce the heat to low, and cook for 30 minutes.

Add the prunes to the skillet, cover, and cook until the veal is tender, about 15 minutes longer. Uncover, taste for seasoning, and adjust as necessary. The sauce should be nicely thickened at this point. If it is not, increase the heat and cook the sauce to desired consistency.

Remove to a warmed platter and serve immediately.

### WHO BUYS TEQUILA?

The United States is far and away the biggest market for tequila, buying up over two-thirds of production, about 4.5 million cases, and growing. Almost one-third of the tequila consumed in the United States is drunk in California.

# SALSAS

The only reason to buy prepared salsa is because it has Paul Newman's picture on it. Just kidding, probably. Salsa has been described as the skeleton that holds Mexican food together. A Mexican table without a bowl of salsa is unthinkable. Don't think of the following salsas as recipes. Think of them as signs, pointing the way to what you can do on your own. Take these salsas and make them something unique to your table. Use proportions and ingredients to please your own palate. A salsa should be a personal statement of the cook, your signature on the meal.

And you can tell that to Paul Newman, too.

While not salsas, the recipes for Here's the Rub and Mexican Cream add two basic tools to your culinary battery. Their uses are described in their respective introductions.

# FRESH TOMATO SALSA
## *Salsa Fresca*

 MAKES ABOUT 1½ CUPS

Try this fresh and flavorful salsa as a dip for chips, folded into guacamole, on top of quesadillas, or as a garnish for the Avocado-Tequila Cream Soup on page 56. You needn't be too precise in the measurements. Add more tomato, use *jalapeños*, or whatever you want. Make it yours.

> 1 large, ripe tomato, finely diced
> 2 green onions, minced, including some of the green tops
> 1 fresh serrano chili, stemmed, seeded, and minced
> ¼ cup cilantro leaves
> juice of 1 lime
> salt

Combine the tomato, green onions, and chili in a small bowl. Stir to mix. Fold in the cilantro and lime juice. Season to taste with salt. This will keep in the refrigerator for 1 day but is best used immediately.

# TOMATILLO SALSA
## *Salsa Verde*

 MAKES ABOUT 2 CUPS

Great as a sauce with grilled meats or fish, or used as a dip for tortilla chips.

> *12 tomatillos, about 1½ pounds total weight,*
> *   husks removed*
> *1 onion, quartered*
> *½ cup cilantro leaves (about ½ small bunch)*
> *1 clove garlic*
> *1 fresh serrano chili, stemmed*
> *½ teaspoon salt*

Put all the ingredients except the salt into a saucepan. Add water to cover generously. Bring to a boil, reduce the heat to medium, and cook, uncovered, until the onion and tomatillos are soft, about 10 minutes.

Using a slotted spoon, remove the solids to a blender. Purée until smooth. Add the salt and whirl to mix.

Taste for seasoning. Pour into a nonreactive bowl and let cool at room temperature before serving. This can be kept in the refrigerator for about 2 days.

# CABBAGE SALSA
*Salsa de Repollo*

 MAKES ABOUT 3½ CUPS

A friend and accomplished cook, Carmen Guttierrez, gave us this recipe. Traditionally it is served with fish, but her family prefers it with grilled or stewed pork.

> 1 small head cabbage
> juice of 1 orange
> juice of 1 lime
> 1 teaspoon salt
> 2 teaspoons sugar
> 1 tablespoon silver tequila
> 1 teaspoon crumbled dried oregano
> 1 large ripe tomato, cut into ¼-inch dice
> 1 canned jalapeño chili, minced, or more if you like your salsa really hot

Remove and discard the tough, outer leaves and the hard core of the cabbage. Finely shred the cabbage with a thin-bladed knife or in a food processor fitted with a slicing disk. Put the cabbage in a nonreactive bowl.

Add the orange and lime juices, salt, sugar, tequila, and oregano. Stir to combine. Stir in the tomato and *jalapeño*. Cover and set aside at room temperature for 30 minutes.

Drain off excess moisture and serve. This can be kept in the refrigerator for up to 3 days.

# TEQUILA SALSA
## *Tequila Chile Salsa*

You can find some variation on this delicious sauce throughout the west-central highlands of Mexico, from sea to mountain. It's used on fish, chicken, beef—just about anything. It keeps tightly covered in the refrigerator for several weeks.

*4 dried* ancho *chilies*
*4 dried* guajillo *chilies*
*1 teaspoon ground cumin*
*½ teaspoon ground coriander*
*1 onion, quartered*
*grated zest of 1 orange*
*2 tablespoons fresh orange juice*
*1 tablespoon silver tequila*
*salt*

Put the chilies, cumin, coriander, onion, and orange zest in a pot. Cover with water by about 2 inches. Bring to a boil, reduce the heat to medium, and cook, uncovered, until the chilies are soft, about 15 minutes. Remove from the heat. Lift out the chilies, reserving the liquid, and, when cool enough to handle, remove and discard the stems and most of the seeds.

Combine the chilies and cooking liquid in a blender with the orange juice and tequila. Purée until smooth. Sieve to remove any remaining skins and seeds.

Season to taste with salt. Can be served warm or at room temperature.

# HERE'S THE RUB
*Marinada con tequila*

 MAKES ABOUT 1 CUP

Rub this garlicky mix onto chicken or chicken pieces before baking or grilling, or use as a marinade. This also makes an excellent marinade for any cut of pork, beef, or lamb. The longer the rub is left on the meat, the more flavor it will impart. It is also good on shrimp or fish, but they shouldn't be left to marinate for longer than an hour for best results. You can keep this in a covered jar in the fridge for several weeks.

*6 large cloves garlic, mashed*
*2 tablespoons silver tequila*
*1 tablespoon paprika*
*1 teaspoon ground cumin*
*1 teaspoon salt*
*1 teaspoon freshly ground black pepper*
*1 teaspoon red pepper flakes*
*½ cup corn or canola oil*
*½ cup chopped red onion*

Combine all the ingredients in a blender. Whirl until smooth. Allow to rest for 1 hour before using.

# MEXICAN CREAM
## *Crema Mexicana*

The ubiquitous sour cream that smothers many Mexican restaurant dishes in North America is seldom encountered in Mexico itself. When cream is used there, it is this slightly tart cream similar to French *crème fraîche*. Once tasted, this cream will slide into your other, non-Mexican, preparations.

> 1 cup heavy cream
> 1 tablespoon sour cream

Put the cream and sour cream in a lidded jar. Cover the jar and shake it until the creams are thoroughly combined. Leave the jar in a warm place for about 24 hours, or until it is very thick and a little sour tasting.

Refrigerate until needed. The cream will keep for about 1 week.

# DESSERTS

Tequila can be used in dessert recipes in the same way you would use brandy or rum. It adds its own distinctive flavor and gives some old favorites a refreshing new taste.

One of our favorite ways to use tequila as a dessert is straight from the glass. The better tequilas can be served as an after-dinner drink in the same way as a fine brandy is. The tequila should be served in a snifter or a large wineglass so the aromas can be appreciated.

# TEQUILA BREAD PUDDING
## Pudín de Pan con Tequila

 SERVES 6

This is more likely to be made with brandy or rum than tequila in Mexico, but we served it to some Mexican friends who fell in love with the taste. Using a very good *añejo* tequila is what gives this dish its deep, rich, satisfying flavor.

> ⅔ cup sugar
> 4-inch-long piece of day-old French bread without crusts,
>     cut into slices ½ inch thick
> 2 tablespoons butter, melted
> ½ cup raisins
> ½ cup chopped pitted prunes, dried apricots, or dried
>     pitted cherries
> 2 cups milk
> 3 eggs, beaten
> ½ cup añejo tequila
> ¼ cup orange-flavored liqueur
> 1 teaspoon vanilla extract
> sweetened whipped cream (optional)

Heat a heavy skillet over medium-high heat. Add ⅓ cup of the sugar and cook until the sugar melts and becomes a deep gold. Very carefully pour the melted sugar into an 8-inch round baking pan. Immediately rotate the pan to spread the melted sugar over the bottom and up the sides of the pan. Let cool.

Put the bread slices in the sugared pan and drizzle the melted butter evenly over the bread. Scatter the raisins and prunes over the top.

In a pitcher or bowl, stir together the milk, eggs, tequila, liqueur, and vanilla extract. Pour over the bread and fruit. Let stand at room temperature for 30 minutes.

Meanwhile, preheat an oven to 350°F.

Put the pudding pan into a larger baking pan. Pour hot water into the larger pan to come halfway up the sides of the pudding pan. Put in the oven and bake until firm, about 1 hour.

Remove the pudding from the oven and from the larger pan. Let rest for 10 minutes. Run a knife around the edge of the pudding to loosen it from the pan. Invert a plate over the pudding and then, holding the plate and pan together firmly, invert them. Lift the pan off of the pudding.

We prefer to serve the pudding warm, but it is also good at room temperature. Never serve it cold from the refrigerator, however. Whipped cream or Mexican Cream (see page 107) makes a nice topping.

# CHOCOLATE-HAZELNUT
# TEQUILA CAKE
### Pastel de Chocolate y Avellanas con Tequila

MAKES ONE 8-INCH CAKE

This is not an everyday cake, but one that would be made only for a special occasion, like a family reunion or a first communion party.

*½ cup (¼ pound) unsalted butter*
*1 cup semisweet chocolate chips*
*⅓ cup hazelnuts*
*6 eggs, separated*
*½ cup granulated sugar*
*⅓ cup gold tequila*
*1 teaspoon ground cinnamon*
*1 teaspoon vanilla extract*
*¾ cup all-purpose flour*
*½ cup raisins*
*powdered sugar*
*1 recipe Carmela's Fruit Salad (optional, see page 61)*

Preheat an oven to 350°F.

Melt the butter in a small saucepan over medium-low heat. Stir in the chocolate chips, remove from the heat, and let the chocolate melt. Stir to make sure all the chocolate melts. Let cool.

Spread the hazelnuts on a baking sheet. Put in the oven until they darken, 12 to 15 minutes. Remove the nuts from the oven and, when they are cool enough to handle, rub the nuts between your palms to remove the loosened skins. It's not necessary to get every speck of skin off the nuts. Coarsely chop the nuts and set aside.

In a bowl combine the egg yolks and granulated sugar. Using an electric mixer on high speed, beat until thick, about 5 minutes. Beat in the cooled chocolate, tequila, cinnamon, and vanilla until well mixed. Stir in the flour, raisins, and chopped nuts.

Line the bottom of an 8-inch springform pan with waxed paper cut precisely to fit. Butter the top of the paper and the sides of the pan. Pour the batter into the prepared pan.

Bake until a toothpick inserted in the center of the cake comes out clean, about 50 minutes. Remove the cake from the oven and put on a rack to cool for 30 minutes. Remove the sides of the pan and let cool completely.

Transfer the cooled cake to a serving plate. Dust lightly with the powdered sugar. If desired, serve the cake with the fruit salad. It makes a wonderful combination.

We were driving the backroads in search of the truth about tequila and, incidentally, a good bowl of *birria*. Our destination was the Molina ranch, some three hours from Guadalajara, near the end of a dirt road turned to a virtual mudslide by days of rain. We had not really thought we would find the truth about tequila there, but, as is the habit with truth, it turned up when least expected. Around us, the green, pleasant fields of corn and wheat stretched up toward the denser, richer blue-green of the hills of Michoacán, where new plantations of agave were growing.

The Molina ranch is a collection of buildings that look a bit like an abandoned 1950s motel somewhere in west Texas. There is a rambling collection of small houses, held together by interspaced open-air sheds, roofed over with tin where most of the real living takes place. Inside each unit there is a lean-to, dirt-floored kitchen, then there are a few steps up to a section of the house with tiled floors, variously divided, but usually into a series of small bedrooms.

The ranch yard was crowded with farm machinery, chickens, goats, cows, horses, and small children. The matriarch of the Molina family, Maria Luisa, met us at the door with a cold beer and a warm embrace. We hadn't seen one another in months, and there was much talk of absent family and friends. Maria Luisa and her husband, Manuel, have raised nine children on the ranch; they now range in age from six to thirty-two years. Of those nine children, five have worked in the United States and two now live there permanently. The fact that Maria Luisa does much of her cooking on a modern propane stove and that she has a refrigerator and a washing machine can be attributed to the money orders she receives fairly regularly from her two daughters in California.

Yet those modern appliances seem tacked on. The real focus, the heart of the kitchen, remains the stone hearth in a nitty-gritty corner of the room. There is no chimney for the waist-high hearth, simply an opening in the tin ceiling. Beside the hearth there is usually a broody hen, sitting on a clutch of eggs or on tiny baby chicks too young to enter into the hardscrabble life of the ranch yard.

It is at the hearth that the real cooking goes forward. That's where the corn is ground, using a stone rolling pin that could be two thousand years old or bought yesterday at a trendy Los Angeles shop. The tortillas pour forth in seemingly endless supply. Seeing Maria Luisa and her three resident daughters-in-law at work around the hearth, one is reminded that the origins of the word *hearth* can possibly be traced back to the Sanskrit word for breath. At the Molina ranch, the hearth is the "breath" of the family.

After some talk of absent grandchildren, we got around to the goat, or more exactly, baby goat: *chivo* on the hoof, *cabrito* on the table.

We had driven several hours to visit the Molinas and to sample what we had been promised by Anita Torres, Maria Luisa's daughter in California, was the best *birria* in Mexico. *Birria* (see page 94) is that wonderful, sometimes difficult-to-translate Mexican dish made of steamed meat (usually goat) served with an intense, dark brown sauce. This is a country dish that has gone to town and become so popular there are cafes called *birriarias* all over Mexico. But we were looking for its country roots at the Molina ranch, and we found them. We also wanted to see if, in any sense, those roots were entangled with the roots of tequila.

But first, you need a goat. For reasons I never understood, the resident Molina goats were not good *birria* material. We climbed into a pickup with Manuel, Maria Luisa's youngest son, and drove a couple of miles in the mud to the foot of the mountains. There stood a huddle of small houses called Rancho Blanco.

Manuel drove the pickup as far as it could go, then we got out and walked several hundred yards up a rocky path until we came, unexpectedly, upon a rather modern-looking house and a quiet-spoken man who, it seemed, had goats. Somewhere. Up on the mountainside he had plenty of goats. Good *birria* stock. He sent several small children up into the brush for the goat.

We returned with the goat to Molina ranch, where Manuel's Uncle, Miguel, the family butcher, was waiting. The only tool he needed was a folding knife with a pointed blade perhaps four inches long. The goat was admired by the children before being taken to a side yard and killed as quickly and as painlessly as killing can ever be done, one supposes. It was held between the butcher's legs, head down with the neck bent back. Miguel felt carefully in the neck for the artery, while a small boy of ten or twelve stroked the goat, calming it with soft words. He found the artery and cut quickly. Manuel held a bucket to catch the spurting blood. Not a drop was lost. It would be boiled overnight and served the next morning as the sauce for tripe tacos with freshly made corn tortillas.

Meanwhile, the extended family had gathered and a few neighbors stopped by. As the night came on, the rain returned in earnest, lashing the tin roof. A spectacular show of lightning and thunder rolled down from the mountains, but we were as snug as could be, with half-gallon bottles of tequila on the table, along with brandy, a local *aguardiente* (made from sugarcane), and beer. A short length of cane had been put in the tequila to satisfy the Mexican sweet tooth.

When the *birria* arrived, the children ate first, seeking out the laps of uncles and aunts, cousins, mothers and fathers. They each clutched a plate of food in one hand and a hot tortilla in the other. Eating and smiling, they almost forgot that we were gringos.

After the *birria*, the guitars were brought out, along with a fresh supply of tequila, and we celebrated the goat.

# INDEX

# TABLE OF EQUIVALENTS

*The exact equivalents in the following tables have been rounded for convenience.*

| US/UK | Metric |
|---|---|
| oz=ounce | g=gram |
| lb=pound | kg=kilogram |
| in=inch | mm=millimeter |
| ft=foot | cm=centimeter |
| tbl=tablespoon | ml=milliliter |
| fl oz=fluid ounce | l=liter |
| qt=quart | |

## Weights

| US/UK | Metric |
|---|---|
| 1 oz | 30 g |
| 2 oz | 60 g |
| 3 oz | 90 g |
| 4 oz (¼ lb) | 125 g |
| 5 oz (⅓ lb) | 155 g |
| 6 oz | 185 g |
| 7 oz | 220 g |
| 8 oz (½ lb) | 250 g |
| 10 oz | 315 g |
| 12 oz (¾ lb) | 375 g |
| 14 oz | 440 g |
| 16 oz (1 lb) | 500 g |
| 1½ lb | 750 g |
| 2 lb | 1 kg |
| 3 lb | 1.5 kg |

## Liquids

| US | Metric | UK |
|---|---|---|
| 2 tbl | 30 ml | 1 fl oz |
| ¼ cup | 60 ml | 2 fl oz |
| ⅓ cup | 80 ml | 3 fl oz |
| ½ cup | 125 ml | 4 fl oz |
| ⅔ cup | 160 ml | 5 fl oz |
| ¾ cup | 180 ml | 6 fl oz |
| 1 cup | 250 ml | 8 fl oz |
| 1 ½ cups | 375 ml | 12 fl oz |
| 2 cups | 500 ml | 16 fl oz |
| 4 cups/1 qt | 1 l | 32 fl oz |

## Oven Temperatures

| Fahrenheit | Celsius | Gas |
|---|---|---|
| 250 | 120 | ½ |
| 275 | 140 | 1 |
| 300 | 150 | 2 |
| 325 | 160 | 3 |
| 350 | 180 | 4 |
| 375 | 190 | 5 |
| 400 | 200 | 6 |
| 425 | 220 | 7 |
| 450 | 230 | 8 |
| 475 | 240 | 9 |
| 500 | 260 | 10 |

## Length Measures

| | |
|---|---|
| ⅛ in | 3 mm |
| ¼ in | 6 mm |
| ½ in | 12 mm |
| 1 in | 2.5 cm |
| 2 in | 5 cm |
| 3 in | 7.5 cm |
| 4 in | 10 cm |
| 5 in | 13 cm |
| 6 in | 15 cm |
| 7 in | 18 cm |
| 8 in | 20 cm |
| 9 in | 23 cm |
| 10 in | 25 cm |
| 11 in | 28 cm |
| 12 in/1 ft | 30 cm |